THE GRIZZLY

The remarkable account of the leading animal of North America, by the no less remarkable creator of Glacier and Rocky Mountain National Parks.

Enos Mills' observations and intimate knowledge of this magnificent beast have never been equalled. For a lifetime he trailed grizzlies, without a gun, across the ranges, plateaus and passes of the Rocky Mountains. Observing them without interfering, he caught unusual glimpses of their way of life. These were animals who slid down snow banks or played hide-and-seek with their shadows for the sheer joy of it, gazed at sunsets and shooting stars for the wonder of it, and followed their all-consuming curiosity, often with hair-raising results. Mothers and cubs, "good" tamed bears and "outlaw" grizzlies, followed Enos Mills as often as he followed them—with high intelligence, and with power, dignity and resourcefulness that are an inspiration to men.

THE GRIZZLY

OUR GREATEST WILD ANIMAL

Enos A. Mills

With an Afterword by

R. L. Grosvenor

BALLANTINE BOOKS • NEW YORK

Copyright 1919 by Enos A. Mills

Renewal Copyright 1947 by Esther Burnell Mills

Introduction Copyright © 1973 by R. L. Grosvenor

SBN 345-03319-1-150

First Printing: June 1973

Printed in the United States of America

Cover photo from F.P.G.

BALLANTINE BOOKS, INC.
201 East 50th Street, New York, N.Y. 10022

Contents

Preface

IT would make exciting reading if a forty-year-old grizzly bear were to write his autobiography. Beginning with the stories from his mother of the long and exciting journey of his ancestors from far-off Asia and of her own struggle in bringing up her family, and then telling of his own adventurous life and his meetings with men and with other animals, he could give us a book of highly dramatic quality. Just what a wise old grizzly would say while philosophizing concerning the white race would certainly be of human interest and rich in material for literature.

A vigorous, courageous adventurer himself, and a keen and constant observer, the grizzly would have clear-cut views concerning the explorers, early settlers, and hunters. The arrival of the early white people aroused his extraordinary inherent curiosity. He watched them with wondering eyes. He was even inclined to walk right into camp to make their acquaintance. He had no evil intentions, but he was greeted with yells and bullets. Relentlessly down through the years he was pursued. Dogs, guns, poison, and traps have swept a majority of the grizzlies away. Their retreat was masterly and heroic, but the odds were overwhelming.

In the midst of this terrible hunt the Yellowstone wild-life reservation was established. Instantly the grizzly understood, years before other big animals did, and in its protection at once came forth from hiding, eager to be friendly with man. I should like to know his wonderings concerning this place of refuge—why its creation, why its mysterious, invisible boundary-lines, and why, outside of it, the fierce, never-ending pursuit for him has still gone on, until his noble species is verging on extinction.

What, too, are his feelings over the increased friendly interest in his species all over the nation? How excitedly must he catch the echoes of discussions which are telling that he has been misunderstood, that he is not a bad fellow! And surely, if writing, he will pause abruptly when he hears that the public, and even the hunter, is making efforts to have the hunt for him checked—learns that there may early be a close season on the grizzly bear.

During the past thirty years I have had numerous experiences with the grizzly bear in various sections of his territory. In it I have camped alone and unarmed. I have trailed the grizzly without a gun. I have repeatedly been outwitted by him, but never has he attacked me. I have not found him ferocious, and I consider him in most respects the greatest animal on the North American continent, if not in the world. He excels in mental development and physical prowess, and he possesses the rare quality of loyalty. He is full of curiosity and is a born adventurer. The species impresses one with its superiority, and the individuality of each grizzly ever stands out.

The material in this book is drawn chiefly from my own experiences with grizzly bears in the wilderness. Ten of the chapters have not before appeared in print. The author acknowledges with thanks the courtesy of the editors of the *Saturday Evening Post* in granting permission to reprint from that magazine parts of three chapters contained in this book; and to the editors of *The American Boy* for two chapters reprinted herein. Dr. C. Hart Merriam has kindly consented to the reproduction of a part of his comment on the grizzly and big brown bears, together with his up-to-date classification of them. This valuable material represents the work of years.

E. A. M.

Grizzly Sagacity

ONE autumn day, while I was watching a little cony stacking hay for the winter, a clinking and rattling of slide rock caught my attention. On the mountain-side opposite me, perhaps a hundred yards away, a grizzly bear was digging in an enormous rock-slide. He worked energetically. Several slabs of rock were hurled out of the hole and tossed down the mountain-side. Stones were thrown right and left. I could not make out what he was after, but it is likely that he was digging for a woodchuck.

After a short time only his shoulders showed above the scattered slide rock as he stood erect. Then he began piling the stones upon the edge of his deepening hole. The slope was steep and the stones had to be placed with care to prevent their tumbling back. After lifting into place one huge slab, he stood and looked at it for an instant and then slightly changed its position. On top of this stone he piled another large one, eyed it closely, shook it to see if it was solid, and finally shifted it a trifle. Had he not been wearing a grizzly-bear coat, it would have been easy to believe that a powerful, careful, thoughtful man was eagerly digging that hole.

The keenness of the grizzly's sagacity and the workings of his rare wit were impressed upon me in a photographing experience that I had. Two other young fellows and I thought we could get a near-by photograph of an old grizzly that ranged near us. We entered his territory at three widely separated places and moved in concert toward the centre. We hoped that either one of us would be able to slip up close to the grizzly or else he, in running away, would come close to one of us.

Very soon one of the boys aroused the bear and started him running. The grizzly had evidently scented him half a mile away. Running in my direction, when within about a mile he discovered my presence, turned, and retreated six or seven miles into a remote corner of his territory. In this retreat he did not go within two miles of either of the other fellows.

Realizing that the bear had eluded us, we slightly separated and moved toward him. He did not wait to be cornered in a canyon. Late that day we followed his devious tracks and discovered his movements. We learned to our chagrin that he had doubled back in the canyon and come part way toward us. Then, climbing an out-thrusting ridge where he could see in all directions, he evidently had watched us when we passed up a grassy valley beneath him. After we were in the timber beyond he had descended to the valley. Then the most amazing turn came. Instead of running away in the opposite direction he had followed along close behind us! By the time we discovered all this the day was gone, and so was the bear. He had had an adventure.

Did the grizzly know we were unarmed? He might have used the same tactics in any case. Anyway, he easily kept out of our way, followed our moves, and had, perhaps, enjoyed our unsuccessful efforts.

I would give the grizzly first place in the animal world for brain-power. He is superior in mentality to the horse, the dog, and even the gray wolf. Instinct the grizzly has, but he also has the ability to reason. His ever-alert, amazingly developed senses are constantly supplying his brain with information—information which he uses, and uses intelligently. His powers of scent are exquisite. His ears hear faint sounds; they are continually on scout and sentinel duty. Wireless messages from long distances which his senses pick up are accurately received and their place of origin correctly determined.

The grizzly appears to guide his daily life with plan and forethought. He has the genius for taking pains. He is constantly alert and meets emergencies with brains. The following actions have impressed me with his keen mental processes.

A grizzly cub in Yellowstone Park found a big ham skin—a prized delicacy. Just as the little fellow was lifting it to his mouth a big bear appeared. He instantly dropped the ham skin, sat down on it, and pretended to be greatly interested in watching something in the edge of the woods.

Another young grizzly in the Yellowstone one day found a tin can that was open at one end and partly filled with fish. He raised it in his fore paws and peeped in, then deliberately turned the can upside down and shook it. Nothing came out. He shook again; no result. Then he proceeded just about as you or I might have done. He placed the can on the ground, open end down, and hammered the bottom of the can with a stone until the fish dropped out.

In a zoo one day, a piece of hard-tack that a grizzly bear wanted fell into the hands of a black bear. The black bear dipped the hard-tack in the water and then started to take a bite. Evidently it was too hard. He put it in the water again, and while it soaked gave his attention to something else. While the black bear was not looking, the grizzly, standing on the farther edge of the pool, stirred the water with a fore paw and started the hard-tack toward him on the waves. The instant the first wave touched the black bear he looked around, grabbed the precious hard-tack, which was rapidly floating away, and, pushing it to the bottom of the pool, put one hind foot upon it. How very like the mental processes of human beings!

One day in North Park, Colorado, I came upon the carcass of a cow that wolves had recently killed. It lay in a grassy opening surrounded by willow clumps. Knowing that bears were about, I climbed into the substantial top of a stocky pine near by, hoping that one would come to feast. A grizzly came at sundown.

When about one hundred feet from the carcass the bear stopped. Standing erect, with fore paws hanging loosely, he looked, listened, and carefully examined the air with his nose. The grizzly is eternally vigilant; he appears to feel that he is ever pursued. As the air was not stirring, I felt that he could not scent me in my tree-top perch. It may be, however, that he faintly caught my lingering scent where I had walked round the opening. After scouting for a minute or two with all his keen senses, he dropped on all fours and slowly, without a sound, advanced toward the willow clumps.

In places of possible ambush the grizzly is extremely cautious. He is not a coward, but he does not propose to blunder into trouble. When within thirty feet of the waiting feast this bear redoubled his precautions against surprise and ambush by walking round the carcass. Then, slipping stealthily to the edge of a thick willow clump, he flung himself into it with a fearful roar, instantly leaping out on the other side ready to charge anything that might start from the willows; but nothing started. Standing erect, tense in every muscle, he waited a moment in expectant attitude. Then he charged, roaring, through another willow clump, and another, until he had investigated every possible place of concealment near the carcass. Not finding an enemy, he at last went to the carcass.

When he had feasted for a few minutes he suddenly rose, snarled, and sniffed along my trail for a few yards. He uttered a few growling threats. That a grizzly cannot climb a tree is a fact in natural history which gave me immense satisfaction. But the bear returned to the carcass and finished his feast. Finally, having raked grass and trash over the remains, he doubled back on his trail and faded into the twilight.

Grizzlies often show courage and strategy by hiding and lying in ambush for a pursuing hunter. On one occasion I had been following a grizzly for a number of days, trying to get his photograph at short range. He knew I was in pursuit. Finally, he doubled back on his trail a short distance and crouched behind a log. His tracks as I followed them passed along the other side of this log, and continued plainly ahead of me across the top of a snow-covered moraine. But as I approached the log, the wind stirred the bear's fur and gave me warning.

A grizzly appears to understand that his tracks reveal his movements. I was once following one that had been wounded by a hunter to see where he went and what he did. He circled from his trail and came back to it over logs and rocks, which left no markings, and hid in a clump of fir trees. On seeing this possible place of ambush by the trail, I turned aside and climbed a pine to reconnoitre. When the bear realized that I had discovered him, he made off in anger.

Round the foot of Long's Peak I followed a bear through a shallow snow, hoping to overtake and photograph him. Most of the snow had melted off the logs and boulders. After trailing him four or five miles I came to a boulder where he had climbed up and looked around. Possibly he wished to see how close I was to him; possibly he was deciding just where he would carry out a plan for outwitting me. At any rate, he jumped from the boulder, walked round it, traveled a short distance slowly, then set off on a run, going east. After I had followed his trail for more than a mile, his tracks ceased in a rocky, snowless area where his footprints did not show.

I thought I should find his tracks in the snow on the farther edge of the rocky space; but they were not there. Then, in the snow, I went entirely round the edge of the rocky space without seeing a track. Thinking that possibly the grizzly was hiding in this small rocky area, I at once cautiously circled every place behind which he might be concealed, but without finding him.

Out in the snow I made a larger circle and at last discovered his tracks. Entering the rocky space, he had turned abruptly to the left and traveled about one hundred feet. Then, from the rocks, he had made a long leap into a clump of bushes, from this leaped into another clump of bushes, and finally into the snow. He thus left the rocky place without leaving any telltale tracks within thirty feet of it.

He started westward—back toward the boulder—

alongside his first trail, and traveled for about a mile parallel to it and less than one hundred feet from it. Near the boulder he waited in concealment at a point where he could watch his former trail, and evidently stayed there until I passed.

Then he traveled on a short distance to another small rocky area. Doubling in his tracks, he came back for one hundred feet or so in the trail he had thus made. Working toward his first trail, he hid his tracks by leaping among fallen timbers and bushes, and at last made a leap into his first trail by the boulder, where he made many tracks in the snow. Along this old trail he traveled east again a short distance, stepping precisely in his former footprints.

Out of this trail he leaped upon the top of a low, snowless boulder on the right, and from this upon another boulder. He walked along a bare fallen log. Here I must have searched more than two hours before detecting two or three broken sticks, which gave me a clue to the direction he had taken. From the log he walked upon a cross log and then plunged through fifty or sixty feet of thicket which showed no trail. From where he had emerged on the farther side of the thicket there was little by which to trace him for the next quarter of a mile. He zigzagged over fallen logs and leaped upon snowless boulders until he came to a tree leaning against a cliff. Up this tree he walked to a ledge, where, fortunately, there was a little snow which recorded his track. He followed the ledge to the top of the cliff and, leaving this, ran for four or five miles. It took me twenty-four hours to unravel the various tangles, and I finally gave up the idea of photographing him. Long before I arrived at the top of the cliff I had concluded that I was following a reasoning animal, one who might be more alert than I myself.

Though a grizzly has both speed and strength, he generally uses his wits and thus obtains the desired end in the easiest way. Three or four persons have told me that they have seen instances of a grizzly bear's taking the part of an acrobat. The bear, by this means, endeavored to attract the attention of cattle, with the idea of drawing them close and seizing one of them. Among his pranks he turned an occasional somersault, rolled over and over, and chased his tail.

A Utah grizzly killed about one thousand head of cattle in fifteen years. During this time there was a large reward offered for his death. Numerous attempts were made to capture him. Old hunters and trappers tried with rifles and traps; expeditions of men, horses, and dogs pursued him. All these years he lived on as usual in his home territory, made a kill every few days, and was seen only two or three times.

Another grizzly, eluding pursuers, slaughtered live stock freely, and managed to survive thirty-five years of concerted efforts to kill or capture him. There was a rich reward on his head.

There are similar accounts of Clubfoot, Three-Toes, and other outlaw grizzlies. All of these bears slaughtered cattle by the hundreds in their home territory, lived with heavy prices on their heads, and for years outwitted skillful hunters and trappers, escaping the well-organized posse again and again. Knowing many of the hunters and their skillful methods, and the repeated triumphs of other grizzlies over combinations and new contrivances, I am convinced that the grizzly bear is an animal who reasons.

When in a trap or cornered, a wounded grizzly sometimes feigns death. Apparently he considers his situation desperate and sees in this method the possibility of throwing his assailant off guard. Considering that need of feigning death is recent—since the arrival of the white man with high-power rifle and insidious steel trap—this strategy appears like a clear case of reasoning.

The grizzly is difficult to anticipate. His strategy usually defeats the hunter. One wounded bear may at once charge the hunter; the next may run from him; and the third may hold the ground defiantly. The grizzly meets what to us seem identical situations in unlike manner, and makes sudden changes in his habits without our seeing the cause for such changes. Quickly he makes the acquaintance of the new and promptly adjusts himself to it. If it is dangerous he avoids it, if advantageous he uses it.

Often in traveling to a distant place the grizzly goes on the run, but just as often he goes at slower speed. If plodding slowly, he conveys the impression of deliberating. He often appears to be thinking, and probably is. Though shuffling along, he is bound for a definite place with the intention of doing a definite thing. Suddenly he changes his mind and goes off in the opposite direction.

I have seen a bear hustling along, with his mind apparently made up; he is in a hurry to carry out some plan, to reach a given place, or see some particular thing. All at once he notices where he is and stops. He remembers that he intended to look at such and such a thing on the way but has neglected to do so. He hesitates a few moments, then goes back.

On rare occasions the grizzly walks along, perhaps in bountiful summer, thinking of nothing in particular, with head swinging slowly from side to side. Something arouses him; he may promptly retreat or he may investigate. You never know what a grizzly will do next or how he will do it, but everything he does is with fresh interest and delightful individuality.

An old grizzly pursued by wolves once gave me a fearful exhibition of nature. He came running across an opening in the southern end of North Park with several wolves close in pursuit. He acted as though away from home—hard pressed, bewildered, and in a strange territory. The wolves were crowding him closely as he reached the edge of the woods. With a sudden move he wheeled and struck at the one in the lead. Instantly the others were around him, snarling and snapping. The grizzly wheeled and struck quickly to right and left, striking outward and downward somewhat after the fashion of a cat striking at a near-by object. Then he turned and ran on.

A few miles farther on he again crossed an opening. Fresh wolves were now in pursuit. I saw several of the pack lying down, panting and resting. The grizzly had no rest, he was hard pressed. At one place, closely crowded, he backed up in the corner of a cliff and here put up such a fight that he drove the wolves off for the time being. He killed one and badly injured two of them. Towards evening he took refuge in a denlike place for which he evidently had been heading. The following morning a number of the wolves were gone, but the others were waiting for the grizzly in front of the den.

A grizzly with three feet managed to maintain himself in a territory near my home, and I twice heard of his outwitting hunters and their hounds.

The territory was occasionally invaded by trappers but he avoided their snares. Hunters with dogs finally drove him off his domain. Where he went, what struggles he had, what masterly retreats he made, what troubles he had in making a living, and what his final tragic end, I do not know. That he survived so long with one foot gone indicates that he was a bear of powers, a bear with a career, whose biography or autobiography would be full of action and adventure.

It cannot be stated too strongly that the grizzly is not a coward. Every drop of blood in his body is courageous. He has no fear. He is intelligent enough to know that man is a dangerous enemy—that it is almost suicidal for a bear to expose himself to man. There is no animal of the wilds whom he avoids. Man, with field-glasses, dogs, and a rifle that will kill at the distance of a mile, are odds too great for him. He wisely endeavors to avoid man, but if he cannot do so, when the fight comes he exhibits one hundred per cent of courage and efficiency.

Only a few generations ago the grizzly was instinctively courageous, never avoiding a foe; with courage he met every issue, almost invariably coming out triumphant. But when man is the issue, the grizzly, seeing more than one move ahead, has the wisdom and the greater courage to suppress the old instinctive trait, for its use would be ineffective.

For years I have watched, studied, and enjoyed the grizzly, have seen his actions under a variety of influences—fighting and playing, sleeping and food-getting. I have watched him when he was under normal influences and abnormal ones; when pursuer and when pursued; have kept him within the focus of my field-glasses for hours at a time, and have trailed for days with a camera this master animal.

The grizzly is so dignified and so strangely human-like that I have felt degraded every time I have seen him pursued with dogs. A few times I have outwitted him; more often he has outwitted me. We have occasionally met unexpectedly; sometimes each stared without alarm, and at other times each fled in an opposite direction. Sometimes the grizzly is guided by instinct, but more often his actions are triumphantly directed by reason.

Cubs and Mother

THE life-story of every bear is a story of adventure. A hunter with whom I was camping in the No-Summer Mountains of Colorado came in one June evening with the report that he had killed a mother grizzly. He had searched for her cubs, which he thought must be near by, but had failed to discover them. The hunter said he had come upon her unexpectedly in a thicket and she had at once charged, probably thinking herself cornered. One well-aimed shot in the head had dropped her.

The following morning I went with the hunter to bring in the grizzly. She was a beautiful silver-tip of about four hundred pounds. We made another thorough search for the cubs without finding them. Just as the hunter was about to start skinning the bear I caught sight of a cub peeping from beneath large slide rocks not thirty feet away. Then another frightened cub face appeared.

After hesitating for a moment both cubs came out and stood looking intently toward us and their dead mother. After a stare, as we did not move, they took a few steps toward us. Hesitating again, they stopped, rose up and looked around, and then hastily retreated to the rocks. Evidently their mother had trained them to stay wherever she left them until she returned.

But they had waited long. For a while they stood and whimpered very much like hungry, forsaken children. They could scent their mother, and see her, too, and were too hungry and lonesome to endure without her longer. Again they started slowly toward us, walking closely side by side. When very near they paused, rose on hind legs, and looked intently at us and in wonder and longing at their lifeless mother. Then they went to her. One little cub sniffed in a bewildered, puzzled way over her cold, still body. He gently stroked her fur with his paw and then sat down and began to whimper and cry.

The other little cub stood looking with awe into his mother's moveless face, but at last shook off his fright and smelled her bloody head. Then, all forlorn, he turned to look eagerly into the face of the hunter, who had been watching the little cub all this while with big tears upon his cheeks. After a moment he took a step toward him, rose up, and trustingly put fore paws upon his knee, looking seriously, confidingly into his face. We carried these little orphans to camp, and the hunter raised them. Their mother was the last animal that he ever shot.

The cubs are born in the hibernating cave in January, February, or March, probably the majority in February. The number at birth commonly is two, but sometimes there are three and occasionally even four. Each is about the size of a chipmunk, weighing from ten to twenty ounces.

Generally the mother does not come forth for either food or drink for some weeks after the cubs are born. She stays in the den a month longer than bears without cubs. Curled around the little bears in the den, she nourishes them from her store of fat. The cubs grow slowly, and on leaving the den are often only a trifle larger than a cotton-tail rabbit, weighing from ten to fifteen pounds. The grizzly appears to give birth to cubs only every second year. Though yearlings have been seen with a mother and cubs, it is likely that they did not belong to her.

In proportion to the size of the mother, the grizzly is one of the smallest of animals at birth, weighing about one fifth of one per cent of her weight. A baby kangaroo at birth is even smaller proportionally, however, and is said to weigh less than one tenth of one per cent of the mother's weight. A baby blue whale is about four per cent of the weight of the mother and sometimes weighs three tons and has a length of twenty-five feet.

Why is the young grizzly so small? It will readily be seen that while hibernating, neither eating nor drinking for a few months, the mother grizzly would not be able to nourish two or more very lusty youngsters. It is probable that in the process of evolution Nature selected the small grizzly cubs to perpetuate the species.

While visiting the Blackfeet Indians in western Montana one February, I saw a young Indian woman nursing two baby grizzly bears. The mother grizzly had been killed a day or two before and the cubs taken from the den. They were little bits of warm, pink life, scantily covered with hair. Each weighed not more than one pound. They were blind and toothless, but had sharp tiny claws. They had their eyes open in about fourteen days, and early began to cut their teeth. For several days the Indian woman suckled the cubs, then she fed them on cow's milk and succeeded in raising them.

Many are the colors of grizzlies. I once saw a mother with four cubs, each of a different color. She herself was cream-colored, but one of the cubs was nearly black, another gray, the third brown, and the fourth black and white. A grizzly may be a blond, or a brunette, or one of half a dozen inbetween shades. Often, as he ages, he becomes a "sil-ver-tip." Probably dark gray is the prevailing color.

From the time the mother and cubs emerge from the winter den in the spring until they enter a den to hibernate the next winter, they are on the move much of the time. Only occasionally does the old bear leave the cubs behind, and this as a rule is not for long. She is constantly watchful for their safety and makes haste to place herself between the cubs and any possible danger. In retreating she usually leads the way, the cubs following closely, but if nearly cornered she is likely to act as rear guard.

Crossing the mountains one stormy spring day, I paused in a whirl of mist and wet snow to look for the trail. Peering ahead, I beheld a grizzly bear emerging from the gloom only a few yards away. Close behind her were two small cubs. Mother Grizzly, as much surprised as I, instantly retreated. With an impatient expression and a growl of anger she wheeled quickly about and boxed the cubs right and left like a nervous mother. Urged on with spanks from behind, the youngsters turned back in the direction they had come from, and all vanished in the falling snow.

Though gentle and patient, the grizzly mother uses a limited amount of cuffing and spanking with the cubs, especially if they are in danger. One day from far across a canyon I was watching two cubs walking along a wild-life trail in front of their mother, when a pack outfit appeared on my side of the canyon. The mother and the cubs saw it, and she at once turned up a gulch, pushing the cubs before her. But the youngsters were interested in the pack-animals and, standing still, forgot every-thing in their eager watching. The mother went from one to the other, pushing them forward. The instant she left one, the cub stopped and turned to look back in eager curiosity at the strange sight across the canyon. Without any show of temper the mother pushed one ahead a few yards and then returned to the other and urged it forward.

The mother protects her cubs at any cost. Many a grizzly mother has died in defense of her offspring, and I do not know of an instance of a mother's running away when her cubs were exposed to danger.

At Grand Lake, Colorado, one June day, I went with a trapper on his rounds, thinking that he might have trapped a grizzly. He had a cub trapped by a fore paw. As we approached the spot, I chanced to climb over a pile of fallen timber and from the top of this I saw Mother Grizzly lying in wait a short distance in front of the cub. She had dug out a place behind a log and was lying there concealed, unmistakably waiting for the trapper.

One morning late in May, while I stood behind a tree watching two young beaver at play in the pond, a small grizzly cub, of the same brown color as the beaver, walked out to the end of a log that lay partly in the water. He was interested in the beaver. Reaching down, he touched the water with right fore paw, whimpered, but hesitated about going in. While he stood looking trustingly at them, the beaver, who had been watching him, dived into the pond.

Cubs as well as human children sometimes become separated and lost from even the most watchful of mothers. This little cub was so thin and weak that he must have been lost for some days. In the woods a trace of snow that had fallen a day or two before still lingered. This enabled me to backtrack the cub to where he had probably spent a part of the night, about a quarter of a mile up stream from the pond. His tracks showed that he had wandered much.

If I left the cub in the woods it appeared improbable that his mother would find him before he starved, and it was unlikely that I should find her, even though I continued the dangerous business of searching for her. I caught the cub without effort, and, after a few feeble attempts to scratch and bite me, he calmed down, licked my hand, and then began to suck a raisin which I handed him from my pocket. He was a tiny little fellow and could not have weighed more than nine or ten pounds. I carried him to the nearest ranch. The children were glad to have him, and a letter from them some months afterwards told me that "Maverick" was happy in his new home.

From a tree-top perch I once had a good glimpse of bear life, as a mother grizzly with two young cubs stopped by a tree to dig out mice. In the midst of her digging mother grizzly caught a faint scent of me and instantly was all concentration. On tiptoe, motionless as a statue, she stood looking, listening, and gathering information with her nostrils. Then she relaxed, dropped on all fours, and for a moment seemed uncertain as to her next move. One of the cubs concluded to suckle. Instantly the mother knocked him headlong with a side swing of her left fore paw. Such thoughtlessness in the face of possible danger was evidently too much to be excused.

The little cub landed some yards away, tumbling heels over head. He showed no surprise, in fact pretended that this was a part of his plan. The instant he rolled on his feet he sniffed the earth eagerly as though he had made a remarkable discovery and started to dig. Without uncovering a thing he presently raced away to overtake mother and the other cub.

Cubs appear to depend upon mother's milk until they are about six months of age. Before this time they may eat a little solid food now and then, but this is done more out of curiosity and in imitation of mother than from desire. It is likely to be July before they do even this and late August before they eat solid things with any regularity. They are not likely to be weaned until just before denning-up time. The Indians in Alaska told me that sometimes the cubs are not weaned until the second autumn of their lives. This certainly is sometimes true, but I think it peculiar to Alaska.

Comical and cunning the cubs appear as they mimic the mother. When she stands up with fore paws against her breast, looking intently into the distance, the cubs stand up with their paws upon their breasts and look in the same direction. When mother turns or sniffs, these cunning little imitators also turn and sniff. The cubs walk up to a spot where the mother has been sniffing and digging and there sniff and dig. If mother continues digging rather long, they find a place of their own and dig. If mother reaches up and pulls down a fruit-laden limb and takes a bite, they too must pull down a twig of some kind and at least look at it.

Around the shores of Chickadee Pond a mother grizzly and her two cubs spent a July day digging out grass roots, willow roots, and probably also grubs. I watched them for hours. Occasionally one took a mouthful of grass or a bite of blue mertensia. After a while mother waded into the pond; cubs of course followed.

The large yellow pond-lilies were in bloom, and mother went about biting off stalk after stalk, apparently forgetting the cubs. One of them grabbed a lily stem and bit two or three times without cutting it. Finally, leaning back, he pulled it apart. He chewed it a little but didn't seem to enjoy it. Then, holding the lily in one paw, he thrust the great golden bulb into his mouth and ate it with apparent satisfaction. The other little cub after much tugging finally uprooted a lily. He chewed at the four-foot stalk in three or four places. Then, taking the bulb in both fore paws, he ate it as though it were an apple.

It is ever a joy to watch a grizzly and her children. A mother grizzly crossing a lake just south of Long's Peak swam low in the water with a cub sitting contentedly on her back. She came directly towards the shore where I was standing concealed behind trees. As she approached I threw a stone into the water close to her. Wheeling about like lightning, Mother Grizzly started at full speed for the farther shore. The cub tipped over in the water, but hastily took a tail-hold and was towed rapidly away.

I once saw a grizzly and cub walking leisurely along the top of a ridge above timber-line, the cub with long strides following in mother's footprints. There were perhaps six or more inches of snow. I sat still. They were coming almost towards me. Watching carefully with my glass, I noticed that the cub was limping. He suddenly sat down and bawled. The mother, after walking on several steps, turned to look at the cub, who was holding his hind foot between his fore paws and examining his hurt. I heard him whimper two or three times, and finally mother went back. She looked down at the bottom of the foot rather indifferently, then turned and walked on. The cub followed after.

When they passed near me the mother rose suddenly on hind legs, stood with fore paws held against her chest, and looked and looked, and sniffed and sniffed. Little cub, forgetting his sore hind foot, stood up with little paws against his breast, stretched his neck, looked, and sniffed—a perfect little imitation of the mother. She moved off several steps and stopped on the very edge of a precipitous ridge to scout. The cub placed his fore paws against mother's side and from this secure position peeped over and beyond her. But they did not detect me and soon went leisurely on.

Two miles farther I crept as close as I could and paused to watch. The mother was digging, the cub watching eagerly. As her digging continued for some time, he moved away, sniffed two or three times, and then began digging rapidly on his own account. While both were digging, there was a whir of wings and a sweep of shadows, and a flock of white ptarmigan alighted among broken ledges near by. While I was watching them, a flock of mountain sheep came along the out-thrusting ridge and paused to play for a few moments on the skyline. In pairs they faced, then reared up and sparred with their horns; they cut lively circles around one another. A rugged, snowy peak loomed grim behind the scene, and the dense forest spread away for miles below. The bears, the ptarmigan, and the sheep, the white peak, the purple forest, and the blue sky gave me a striking experience and left a splendid picture. As I turned to go, the cub was giving all his attention to the play of the sheep.

The almost continual play of the cubs is a never-ending source of interest. They race, they wrestle, they box, and they play hide and seek with utmost enthusiasm. They climb upon mother's back, they swat and pummel her and maul her. She will endure this by the hour with absolute indifference. Mother sometimes plays with the cubs but more often lets them play with her, or, unconcerned, simply watches them in their scrambles.

Playing cubs are strikingly boylike in their ways. They tumble and roll about with lively energy. Their boxing is a ludicrously earnest show. Standing up they clinch, struggle, break away and watch for a new advantage. They strike first with one paw, then with the other, then with both at once. They come close, dodge, and jump back; they hold one paw high and the other low; sometimes they guard the face with one arm while striking with the other. Often they strike wildly, evidently intending to miss; they bristle up, growl, and have great fun, pretending to be more in earnest and terrible than they really are.

No two boys ever had more excitement and fun swimming in a river than did two cub bears whom I once watched. These cubs raced, splashed, and pushed one another under the water. They dived and swam beneath the surface and from a boulder plunged into it with terrific splashes, sometimes forward, sometimes backward.

One of the happiest incidents which I have seen in the grizzly bear world was a mother grizzly who had discovered some honey in a standing dead tree, perhaps five or six feet above the ground. Tearing open the edges of the hole, she helped herself to a quantity of the honey, then called her two cubs, who were playing a short distance away.

They needed no second invitation when they saw mother standing on hind legs and leaning forward with fore paws against the trunk of the tree. Up the incline of her back they raced merrily, and, standing upon mother's head, they ate with eagerness this wonderful feast of honey.

The cubs den up with their mother the winter following their birth. The mother is their companion until they are a year and a half old, sometimes longer. During their second summer she commonly leaves the cub—or cubs, as the case may be—to make their way in the world alone. Once the family ties are broken, the grizzly is seldom seen with other bears.

If two, three, or four in number, the yearlings run together another year, and are chummy and inseparable. One becomes the leader and is followed faithfully. If trouble arises, they are united and devoted little people. To kill or injure one of the youngsters means that a hunter is promptly charged by the others, and often killed or injured.

The cubs are great ramblers. They may wander through unoccupied regions and over the territory of other bears. They are not considered intruders by other bears. There are numerous interesting incidents in the companionship of these year-olds, and sometimes of two-year-olds, who have explored miles of territory, chased animals, played, and enjoyed themselves together, and in moments of danger united and fought the enemy. Yearling bears den up together the second winter and occasionally also the third winter. Generally, however, after the second winter, that is to say, when two and a half years old, they separate. From this time on the grizzly lives alone.

Where does he make his first home? Sometimes

the young grizzly crowds into the territory adjoining his birthplace, but at other times he must wander far away to find territory not already occupied. In the past, when grizzlies were numerous, the increased population each year must have compelled readjustments and forced a reduction of the area claimed by each individual. But in these times, except perhaps in two or three National Parks, there are thousands of square miles here and there over the West without a grizzly on them. But the grizzly is fond of his home territory, and in it, except for occasional visits into the outside world, he spends his life.

His Exclusive Territory

A MOTHER grizzly and her year-and-a-half-old cub came shuffling along the shore of a little lake in the No-Summer Mountains. Where a brook flowed into the lake she stopped, looked at the cub, and possibly grunted something to him. She may have said, "Here, Johnny, is a territory not claimed by other bears; this is to be your domain." I watched him as she went ambling away alone. He stood looking at the ground for several seconds, then turned to see his mother in the distance, and finally surveyed his surroundings. Pushed off into the world to shift for himself, the cub walked up the mountain-side and disappeared in the woods.

I had seen this cub and his mother on the other side of the Medicine Bow Mountains, at least fifty miles away. When I saw her leaving the cub to make his way alone, I wanted to ask, "Is it common for a mother grizzly to take her children to the territory that is to be their home?" The selection of this domain may sometimes be made by the mother but most often, probably, it is made by the cubs.

But, selection of the home territory aside, the grizzly leads a solitary life; he lives apart from other bears, has his thought, his work, his recreation, and his play by himself. Alone he hunts for food, alone he wanders for adventure. Singly he fights his foes, and in solitude he dens up in winter. A possible explanation of this may lie in the fact that being alone is an advantage to an animal of his size and enormous food-requirements. Then, too, since the advent of the white man with the long-range rifle, it is an advantage to act singly. The grizzly's solitary habit may be one which is an advantage in the perpetuation of the species. Only twice have I known of father, mother, and cubs being seen together, and I have never heard of their denning together.

A grizzly has his own home territory. He claims the exclusive use of certain lands. In only one instance have I known two companion grizzlies to occupy the same region permanently. These two were often seen eating, traveling, and resting near each other. Though the grizzly wanders off the home territory for an occasional visit, in it through the seasons and through the years he makes his living; he defends it against invaders, and in it he commonly dies.

Most wild creatures have their home territories, areas which they claim the right to use to the exclusion of others of the same species. The bear is likely to hold more territory than any other kind of life; and he will dominate in the territory all kinds of life that may temporarily conflict with his use of it. Most birds and beasts use their large or tiny bit of earth in pairs, flocks, herds, or colonies. The grizzly uses his alone. His domain may be in part the claimed territory of other species; lions, beavers, wolves, eagles, and other life may use it.

The grizzly bear is the aristocrat of the wilds. He is lordly and reserved. He will meet a bighorn sheep or other wild animal, and, though aware of its presence, pay no apparent attention to it. If near another bear, either a black or a grizzly, while appearing to be disinterested, or pretending not to have seen him, he is in fact watching the other's movements. A black bear avoids him. Sometimes two grizzlies who have been feeding near each other deliberately meet, or come face to face. Each, with admirable acting, feigns intense surprise that the other is there. They bristle up, exchange a few unfriendly roars and growls, make a threatening move or two, and then go on. Sometimes they pass as though unconscious of each other's presence.

A network of trails extends over the grizzly's mountain home. These reach food-supply centres, lookout and resting stations, swimming-holes, and other places often visited. Generally when going anywhere the grizzly follows a trail; if pursued, he is most certain to do so. Many of these trails are dim, but others are deeply worn. He may sometimes make a new trail, but in general he follows the old ones which have been used by generations of bears. His domain may be crossed by other wild-life trails, which he may or may not use.

Topography, mountain barriers, streams, or other natural boundary-lines in part determine the form of the grizzly's home territory. The size is determined by the food-supply, by the bear population of the region, and by individual prowess. A bear of exceptional prowess may hold an empire.

The territory dominated by old "Timberline" had an area of about eighty square miles. The western boundary-line followed the rim of the Continental Divide for nearly fifteen miles. Meeker Ridge and Cony Creek were other boundary-lines, while at the north stood Chief's Head Mountain and Long's Peak. Toward the south the territory narrowed and was not more than two miles across; in the centre it must have been nearly ten miles wide. An extensive area lay above the timber-line. There were forests primeval, a number of cañons and streams, numerous small lakes and beaver ponds. In this varied and extensive region old "Timberline" had all the necessities of life and many of the luxuries of beardom.

The claw-marks and the tooth-marks which grizzlies and some other animals place on trees are often interpreted as being "No Trespass" signs, indications of boundary-lines, survey marks, or the seal of ownership of the landlord. If these marks are extremely high, they are supposed to inspire respect for the one occupying the region, or to cause terror to the invader, unless he be large enough to reach higher. But I question any such significance attached to these marks. Offtimes the bear leaves these marks in the centre of his home range, sometimes within the home territory of a lion or a bighorn. While the idea of its being a mark of ownership is a most artistic and entertaining one, it does not appear to have any natural-history value.

I have seen bears, reaching high, tear out pieces of bark, and have also seen both bears and lions put claw-marks upon trees. Generally this clawing and biting was done during languid and leisurely moments when there was nothing definite to do. One day I watched a grizzly stand on hind feet upon a five-foot snowdrift where he had been lying. Placing his front paws against a spruce as high as he could reach, he clawed the bark indifferently. It was more of a muscle-stretching performance than anything else. He took a tiny bite out of the tree and walked off with the strip of bark in his mouth. Then he gave it a playful shake and dropped it.

It is well known that wolves, beavers, and some other animals have information places. These may or may not be intentionally established. Some of these places are where wild-life trails cross, or are near water-holes, salt-licks, play places, or some neutral feeding-ground. They may be frequented exclusively by one species or by several. Even the casual visits and bark-biting of bears incidentally contribute something of interest to the next visitors. In these places an animal may learn of the recent visit of one of his species or of a dreaded enemy, or may even find information as to the sex of the visitors. They are thus akin to country crossroads where gossip is exchanged concerning human affairs.

A grizzly that I was trailing turned abruptly aside to visit a news station of this kind. Plainly it was a loafing or frequented spot for wild life; from the nature of the topography and from numerous tracks seen during later visits I learned that it was a stamping-ground and a trail-crossing. Foxes, coyotes, skunks, rats, deer, and mountain sheep had been visitors. The manner in which the bear turned aside to visit the place suggested that he had been there before; but he may just have caught interesting, newsy scent which attracted him there for the first time. His actions were those of one who is hunting for news.

At night the bear may lie down in almost any place, but during the daytime he selects one of the safest places in his realm. If in the high mountains this may be on a ridge above the timber-line, or on a treeless hilltop from which he commands a wide outlook, or in the end of a canyon, or in a thicket. Wherever the place, it is one where the bear cannot be easily surprised, and where his scouts—his scent, his sight, and his ears—would easily warn him of the approach of any possible danger.

When pursued, the grizzly tries to keep within his domain. Usually he travels only seven or eight miles in one direction, then doubles back, circles, and zigzags. Only two or three times when trailing the bear have I known him to travel more than fourteen or fifteen miles in one direction. In one long trailing experience I observed that the bear, with many twists and zigzags, covered his domain practically twice over. I trailed the same grizzly two Septembers, three years apart. I started him the second time near the place where I had started him before, and he followed for three days over almost exactly the same route taken the first time.

Three prospectors and I were rowing across a lake in the Sawtooth Mountains of Idaho. When about half a mile from the farther shore, we spied a grizzly swimming across. We pursued, and when we got near, one of the men proposed to rope him, saying that the bear could now tow us ashore. The other two protested so vigorously that the rope was not thrown. Fortunate for us that it was not, for had it fallen over the neck of Mr. Grizzly, the chances are that he might have climbed into the boat. In Alaska I saw a grizzly out at sea, swimming vigorously along between two islands that were seven miles apart. The grizzly is fond of water, is an excellent and enduring swimmer, and in the water fights effectively.

While I was on a winter trip into the San Juan Mountains a prospector told me of an occurrence which he had just witnessed. A snow-slide crashing down into a gulch close to a grizzly den aroused the bear, who came out with a rush to see what was going on. He did not lose his head, but looked about until the air cleared of the swirling snow-dust. Then he walked round the wreckage brought down by the slide and finally climbed it and explored the opening it had smashed through the woods. After being out more than an hour he reentered the den.

Though living a solitary life in the seclusion of the wilderness, this bear was again routed out before spring. His den was only a few feet above the stream, on the mountain-side. The debris brought down by the snow-slide forty or fifty feet up the gulch dammed the stream and raised the water so that it leaked through the earth into the den. Again driven forth from his den, the bear—so his tracks in the snow showed—after one pause climbed to another den on the mountain-side about two miles distant.

The grizzly spends about one third of each year in hibernation. He may use the same den year after year, repairing and reshaping it; or perhaps he will dig a new one. Sometimes he goes outside his own territory for a den to his liking. He is sometimes driven forth during hibernation by landslides as well as by snow-slides and floods.

A grizzly is strongly attached to his home territory and spends most of his time in it. Occasionally, and in exceptional cases regularly, he wanders far away. A scarcity of food may cause him to leave home temporarily; or excessive food elsewhere may attract him.

Bears and lions are not neighborly, and at best each ignores the other; but one bear I knew followed a lion for weeks, and others have occasionally done likewise, profiting by the food-supply— the excessive killing of the lion. Here was unusual tolerance, almost friendly association, between antagonistic wild folk.

The abundance of food at any place in a bear's territory gives other grizzlies public rights. A berry-patch or a stream which has a supply equal to the needs of many bears, a beaver pond, or a lake, may become a public feeding-place. A flood, a storm, a snow-slide, or other agency may take the lives of a number of animals—cause a congestion of food in any territory.

That there sometimes is fighting in these public places, and that one bear sometimes tries to hog a larger food-supply than he can use does not change the custom of the species. Incidentally, this violation of general or public rights but reminds us how human-like are bears in their habits, good and bad.

Lewis and Clark found a number of grizzlies congregated at places along the Missouri River. Apparently these had got together like those in Yellowstone Park, because of congested food-supply. It appears that at regular crossings along the river numbers of buffalo were annually drowned, and carcasses regularly strewn at about the same places.

There are a number of regions in Alaska where a bear lives in his own chosen locality but regularly goes to a public feeding-ground. Much of the food is along the seashore and on the lower courses of streams. There is also a food-belt above the timber-line, where mice abound and where there is grass upon which bears feed. The seasonal nature of part of the food may thus encourage or compel bears of one locality to travel a long distance to secure the only food obtainable.

If there be straggling grizzlies who wander about like gypsies, they are the rare exception: the nearest to them were the few "buffalo grizzlies," those that in old days followed the migrating buffalo herds.

Though the problem of getting a living makes up most of the grizzly's daily programme, he knows the wisdom of taking time off and having a change from the routine of life. The ability to concentrate in eager play is probably one of the best evidences of the grizzly's unusual brain-power. It is good to know that, although most of the time he lives alone and takes things seriously, he also has the power to relax and to build and restore himself in play. This may help to give contentment to solitary life in home territory.

When well fed, the grizzly sometimes strolls over his estate and pauses to watch the antics of other wild life. He will stand in a stream to see the ways of water-ouzels. The sliding of otter at play appears to interest him, and I have discovered otter-slides by following his tracks to them. Once, when I was enjoying the play of a number of beaver racing and splashing in a pond, a grizzly watched them for a time from the edge of the woods, then came out on the dam and sat down where he could better see them. Though a solitary and self-contained baron, he has many entertaining interests.

There are times at home, or abroad, when the grizzly is not deeply interested in anything, when time hangs a little heavy on his hands, or on his mind. Sometimes at home he doesn't quite know what to do with himself. He isn't hungry, he can't think of any place where he cares to go, he isn't interested in swimming, he doesn't even want to play. He doesn't care to lie down and sleep. He starts off languidly, stops, moves on, rears up, takes a bite out of the bark of a tree; but he doesn't care for the bark to eat and doesn't even look up to see how high he has bitten.

The grizzly is a descendant of a long line of wanderers and may occasionally explore surrounding territory for sheer adventure. If much harassed by settlers, he will move to a permanent

home in lands far distant. It would be comparatively easy for a grizzly to become acquainted with
four or five thousand miles of territory. He travels
rapidly, has endurance, and in a single night could
cover a hundred miles or more.

Some bears get the idea of territorial expansion
and go forth to seize a part of a neighbor's hunt-
ing-ground. Thus one bear may be annoyed by another who makes too frequent raids into his
domain, and feel called upon to defend his territory against the invader. When past prime a bear
is sometimes driven forth into an unfriendly world
by a young, vigorous conqueror.

On one occasion I tracked a grizzly for sixty
miles from the margin of its home range. It
traveled along a line that indicated it had a definite place in mind to which it was going. It explored a canyon region, and, a day or two later, as
tracks in the snow showed, went back to its old
range along the trail it had followed in leaving it.

Going one autumn from Estes Park to North Park,
Colorado, I came upon a grizzly's track in the upper end of Forest Canyon. For several miles it had
followed an old wild-life trail. It crossed the Continental Divide, then the No-Summer Mountains.
From its trail I judged that it, too, knew where it
was going.

Had these bears gone to explore, to see the opportunities of a new region? Or had they returned
to old territory which they knew, perhaps to obtain
some particular kind of food, or just to have an
outing? If seeking new domains, it is possible that
they would explore a number of localities before
selecting one.

In a few localities bears migrate in the spring
and return home in the fall. In these migrations the

grizzly breaks his solitary custom and travels in company. Most likely the bears happen to be on the same route at the same time, and, like Pullman passengers, travel together without speaking.

I saw eight grizzly bears one November traveling single file northward from Middle Park. Backtracking, I found that they had come from the mountainous empire around the southern end of this park. They crossed over into North Park in almost a straight line. Were they, I wondered, heading for a new home, or was this an annual foraging affair? The topography of the country traveled had some bearing on the common route taken, but why were they traveling together? I heard of a number of bears traveling together in northern New Mexico.

On one occasion a hunter on No-Wood Creek in the Big Horns saw seven old grizzlies and two cubs together in the autumn. They were back-tracked to the Yellowstone Park. The garbage-dumps in the Park are frequented by neighboring bears and by numbers from outside the bounds of the Park.

As bears age, their teeth become broken and badly worn away. With difficulty they manage to live. They are often handicapped through loss of toes and by other injuries received in accidents and fights, and through a weakening of faculties due to age. Their normal life appears to be from thirty-five to fifty years.

In the mountains of the north of Yellowstone Park I came upon an extremely old, hard-looking bear. I sat for some time within forty feet of him, watching him rip an old log to pieces to get the ants and white grubs. I was so close that I could see his tongue as it busily licked to right and left. His red-looking eyes stared strangely. I think that he must have been nearly blind, and also that he had nearly lost his ability to scent. When I moved a little closer, he stopped eating, rose up, sniffed the air queerly as though endeavoring to catch scent of me, then listened and looked. He was not at all sure of my presence, though looking in my direction. Two or three days later this old bear was killed. Many of his teeth were gone, and others were badly worn away. His claws were extremely blunt. His head and hide showed many scars—marks of fights and marks from numerous bullets.

One February, when I was spending a few days with a prospector, he brought home the interesting news that he had found a dead grizzly bear. The bear evidently had died while hibernating. He was found curled up in his den and frozen solid. He was old, in poor condition, and his insides were swarming with vermin. I once found a fat young grizzly, apparently healthy, who had the appearance of having frozen to death while hibernating. The time was about the middle of January. The winter to date had been extremely cold, and but little snow had fallen.

I have known of other grizzlies who met strange deaths, but, considering the fairly numerous grizzly population at the time when I was wandering the wilds, the number of bodies found is surprisingly small. One of these grizzlies had perished in a forest fire, another in a desert flood, one was killed at the foot of a cliff by a falling stone, and another was crushed in a snow-slide. Just how or where most old grizzlies come to an end, or what becomes of their bones, I have never been able to learn. It may be that many of them die in the winter dens, which cave in and bury the remains. In closing his adventurous career the grizzly appears to conceal the trail to his last resting-place.

Making a Bear Living

GLANCING across a beaver pond one day, I saw a big, grayish grizzly bear walk out into the grassy opening. My presence was not suspected, and I at once focused my field-glasses upon him. Here and there he went. As a grasshopper leaped into the air, the bear—big, fat, awkward, lumbering fellow that he was—leaped into the air after it. Striking the grasshopper with a fore paw, he would knock it to the ground and then pick it up with his teeth. Occasionally he advanced on all fours and slapped his paw upon the grasshopper before it leaped into the air. Once two grasshoppers flew up at the same instant. The bear stood still, located the spot where each had alighted, and then paid his respects to them in turn.

About this time another bear came into the opening within a hundred feet of the scene of activity. He was dark-gray, almost black, in color, but he too was a grizzly. After smelling here and there, the second bear dug out something; I think it must have been a nestful of mice. A minute later in the edge of the tall grass he found a bumblebee's nest. This he ate in its entirety. Apparently two or three of the bees escaped, to judge from the bear's rapid defense of his nose. Occasionally, as he walked about, he ate a huge mouthful of grass, taking three or four bites at a time.

Neither of these bears paid the slightest attention to the other. Though each must have known, from both scent and sight, that the other was near, they very successfully appeared to be oblivious of

37

the fact. A beaver pond is often a neutral feeding and swimming place.

"As hungry as a bear" is an expression of variable meaning. About one third of the year a bear has an omnivorous appetite; for another four months he lives on short rations; and during the remainder of the year he goes on a food strike and hibernates.

A bear spends most of his waking hours making a living. He has simply a devastating appetite, and as his taste runs to small stuff and dainties, he is kept on the move.

If he denned high up the mountain-side his surroundings are likely to be mostly snow-covered when he comes forth in the spring. Under such conditions he travels miles down the mountains to feed on the early plants already started on the lowlands. He may then slowly follow spring and summer in their steady advance up the far-reaching slopes. To a certain extent his movements are determined by the calendar. He feeds upon the best the season affords. He knows when each article of diet is in season and where in his home territory, or out of it, this abounds. In berry time look for a bear in a berry-patch. Like an enthusiastic fisherman he impatiently waits for the open season—spawning-time—and is on hand early to start fishing.

Perhaps it would be well if we could think of the grizzly as being largely vegetarian. He digs up roots; feeds on weeds, tender shoots of shrubbery, fungi, mushrooms, berries, seeds, rose-hips, pine-nuts, and acorns; and also eats bark like a rabbit and grass like a grass-eater.

The aspens were in bloom, laden with swollen buds and juicy catkins. Many birds were feasting on the catkins; and, looking over into a near-by aspen thicket, I saw a grizzly on a ledge also feeding eagerly. Reaching for a limb, first with one fore paw and then the other, he bit off a few inches and ate twigs, bark, and bloom. Occasionally he seized the top of an aspen with both paws, bent it down, and bit it off. It was similar to the fashion followed in eating wild plums and choke-cherries. A bear will reach up and pull down the top of a plum tree, and, biting it off, eat the small limbs, the bark, the leaves, and the fruit. A grizzly browsing in a wild raspberry-patch will bite off the tops of the vines together with the berries, the leaves, and the thorns. Sometimes the twigs and terminal buds of the pine, the fir, and the spruce are eaten.

One day I saw a grizzly approaching in a manner which indicated that he knew exactly where he was going. On arriving at an alder clump by the brook he at once began tearing off the bark and eating it. On another occasion I watched a bear strip nearly all the bark within reach from a young balsam fir. I have often seen places where bears had bitten and torn chunks of bark from aspens and cottonwoods. Though they also tear the bark from pine and spruce trees, I do not believe that this is eaten as frequently as the bark of the broad-leaved trees.

During the first few weeks after coming out of the winter den much of the grizzly's food is likely to be of the salad order—juicy young plant stalks, watery shoots, tender bark, young grasses, buds, and leaves. In late autumn, just before hibernating, his last courses are mostly roots and nuts.

However, the normal grizzly is an omnivorous feeder, refusing only human flesh. He will eat anything that is edible—meat (fresh, stale, or carrion), wasps, yellow-jackets, grasshoppers, ants and their

eggs, bugs, and grubs. Of course he eats honey and
the bees. He also captures snakes, and many a rat
and rabbit. He is a destroyer of many pests that af-
flict man, and in the realm of economic biology he
should be rated high. I doubt if a dozen cats,
hawks, or owls annually catch as many mice as the
average grizzly.

The food of a grizzly is largely determined by locality. Along the streams of the northern Pacific
Coast he lives chiefly upon fish, while the grizzlies
in the Bitter Root Mountains and British Columbia
generally feed upon roots and plants. Those in the
Rocky Mountains of Colorado and the Southwest
have a mixed diet.

The spring-beauty, the dog-tooth violet, and the
shooting-star, both tops and roots, supply the grizzlies of some localities with much of their food,
while in other regions they rarely, and possibly
never, touch them, though they grow abundantly.
The bears in the Bitter Root Mountains eat the
shooting-star freely, while the violet and the
spring-beauty are favored by the bears of the
Selkirks. Yet, strange though it is, the bears of both
localities pay but little attention to carcasses which
they find. One of the plant roots which the bears of
British Columbia dig out in autumn until the
ground is frozen, is a wild pea, the hedysarum.

I frequently followed a grizzly whose home territory was close to my cabin in the Rocky Mountains. Apparently he liked everything. One day he
spent hours digging out mice. On another he
caught a rabbit. He ate a bumblebee's nest, and,
with the nest, the grass, the bees, their young, their
honey, and their stings. In a homesteader's garden
he dug out and ate nearly one hundred pounds of
potatoes and turnips. The homesteader thought

that a hog had been in his garden. In places I too have thought that hogs had been rooting where bears had simply been digging for roots—places with dug and upturned earth often many square yards in extent. They dig out the roots of the wild parsnip, the shooting-star, and grass, the bulbs of lilies, and sometimes the roots of willow and alder.

I endeavored to find out the kind of food preferred by two young bears that I raised. A number of times I approached them with a plate upon which were cake, meat, and honey. In my pockets I generally had also either turnips or apples. When I appeared the bears usually stood on hind legs to see what I had. If they caught the scent of apples or turnips, they thrust paws or noses into my pockets, ignoring the dainties on the plate. Otherwise they grabbed whatever happened to be nearest them on the plate.

All grizzlies appear to be fond of fish. In many places they are most successful fishermen. I watched a grizzly standing in the riffles of an Idaho stream, partly concealed by a willow clump. In half an hour he knocked five large salmon ashore. With a single lightning-like stroke of a fore paw, the fish was flung out of the water and sent flying fifteen or twenty feet. Rarely did he miss. Each of the salmon weighed several pounds.

A grizzly in the Sawtooth region, trying to catch some fish, sprawled out on a low bank by the edge of a stream. Holding himself with one fore paw, he reached over with the other and felt along the bank beneath the water. He did this very much as a fat man might. More frequently the bear makes a stand in driftwood on the bank, or on a log that has fallen into the stream, or behind a willow clump. Sometimes he captures fish by wading up a brook and seizing with claws or teeth those that conceal themselves beneath banks and projecting roots.

A huge brown grizzly mother catching trout for her two fat cubs held my attention one day. The cubs waited on the grassy bank of a brook while the mother brought them trout after trout. She sometimes caught the fish by thrusting her nose into the water beneath the bank or by reaching in with her paws. Occasionally she knocked them out of the water as they endeavored to dash past her in the riffles. The cubs watched her every move; but they were not allowed to enter the water.

Sometimes the grizzly will collect and cover over an excess of carcasses or fish. By a little mountain lake at the headwaters of the Columbia I found a pile of stale salmon beneath a number of large logs and stones. The fish had been caught during spawning-time and stored for future consumption. A day or two later I returned, and tracks showed that the bear had come back and consumed the salmon.

The grizzly eagerly earns his own living; he is not a loafer. Much work is done in digging out a cony, a woodchuck, or some other small animal from a rock-slide. In two hours' time I have known him to move a mass of earth that must have weighed tons, leaving an excavation large enough for a private cellar. I have come upon numbers of holes from which a grizzly had removed literally tons of stone. In places these holes were five or six feet deep. Around the edges the stones were piled as though for a barricade. In some of them several soldiers could have found room and excellent shelter for ordinary defense.

When a large stone is encountered in his digging

the grizzly grabs it with both fore paws, shakes and tears it loose from the earth, and hurls it aside. I have seen him toss huge stones over his shoulder and throw larger ones forward with one paw. Grizzlies show both skill and thought in nearly everything they do. They have strength, alert wits, and clever paws, and commonly work at high speed. Yet they appear deliberate in their actions and work in a painstaking, careful manner.

A grizzly I followed one day paused in a grassy space to dig out mice. In reaching them he discovered a chipmunk's burrow. By the time he had secured all the mice and chipmunks he had torn up several square yards of sod. The place had the appearance of having been rooted up by hogs. In this fresh earth the surrounding trees sowed triumphant seeds, and here a cluster of spruces grew where grass had long held sway.

A grizzly seems never too busy or too hungry to stop and look around. "Safety First" appears to be more on his mind than eating. I have seen a grizzly pause from his earth-digging after roots to stop, look, and listen, and I have watched one stop his more than eager digging after marmots to scent the air in his scout for an enemy. And then again I have repeatedly seen him look up from his feast of smelly sirloin to make certain that he was not surprised by man.

While I was watching a flock of mountain sheep feeding down a slope just above the timber-line, a grizzly appeared on the scene. He came slowly upward from the woods. Unless the sheep or the bear changed course there must be a meeting. But the sheep continued to feed downward and the grizzly to walk up. Suddenly the bear stopped and began digging—digging evidently for a chipmunk. A stream of earth was sent flying behind him. Occasionally, too, a huge stone was sent hurtling back. This activity roused the curiosity of the sheep, and they approached within perhaps ten or twelve feet. They were lined up and eagerly watching the grizzly when he became aware of their presence. Disliking their close approach, he leaped at them with a terrific "Woof!" The sheep scattered wildly but ran only a few yards. Again uniting, they fed quietly away, and the grizzly returned to his digging.

In only exceptional cases has the grizzly been a killer of big game. In his search for food he digs out small mammals and kills rabbits and beaver. He is not likely to attempt anything as large as wild sheep, but when a grizzly forms the habit of killing big animals he is likely to make this serve as his entire food-supply. Thus a cattle-killing grizzly is likely to give his chief attention to the killing of cattle, or incidentally to that of sheep, deer, or elk. In the days of the buffalo the great herds frequently were trailed by one or more grizzlies. These, however, probably obtained most of their meat from carcasses left behind by storms, drowning, or other means of death.

The misfortunes of other animals often provide a feast for the grizzly. In going over an area just swept by a forest fire I saw two grizzlies feasting, and there were feasts for numerous others. One was wading in an abandoned beaver pond and feasting on the dead trout that floated on the surface. Two black bears, despite terrible threats from the grizzly, claimed all the fish that came within reach of the shore, but discreetly kept out of the pond. During the second day's exploration of the burn a bear came upon me while I was eating from a fire-killed, roasted deer. When I moved on, the waiting grizzy walked up to dine.

A grizzly knows the location of every beaver pond in his territory. It is one of his favorite loafing and feeding places. Often he rolls and swims about in the water, enjoying himself immensely. Here he sometimes finds a stale fish or a dead bird brought down by the stream. Sometimes he eats a huge salad of pond-lilies.

But when beaver are gathering the harvest, especially if it is gathered at some distance from the water, he lies in wait and overhauls them. He is ready, too, to seize upon any of these unfortunate fellows who is accidentally killed or injured in gnawing down a tree. Many a time I have seen the fresh tracks of a mother and her cubs on the muddy shore of a beaver pond, and sometimes the tracks of both black bears and grizzlies.

In the course of miles of daily wandering the grizzly may occasionally come upon a wounded animal or a carcass. If his find be large, he may lie close until it is consumed; or he may make a cache of it, returning again and again until it is eaten. Grizzlies will bury an elk in the earth or cover the carcass of a cow with numbers of logs. Nothing is more common than for them to cover a carcass with refuse consisting of twigs, fallen leaves, grass, and trash. They will cover a quantity of fish with stones and logs.

A few grizzlies become cattle-killers; many grizzlies eat cattle they did not kill. On the live-stock ranges in the mountains of the West cattle die from many causes. They succumb to disease and to accidents. Winds proclaim carcass news and a feast to flesh-eaters near and far. Bears have amazingly keen noses and often are the first to enjoy the feast.

A grizzly I was following caught the scent of a carcass that was more than a mile away. He stopped and sniffed, then changed his course and set off for the carcass. The carcass was being watched. As the grizzly was the first animal to arrive after the kill, the owner of the cow concluded that he was guilty of the killing, and accordingly proceeded to kill him and to condemn all bears as cattle-killers. Yet this cow had died from feeding too freely upon poisonous larkspur.

I was once trailing a grizzly through the snow, when he came upon the trail of a mountain lion, which he followed. Farther along the lion killed a horse. When the grizzly came upon the scene, he drove the lion off. The following day, while having a second feast off the horse, he was discovered by a rancher, who at once procured dogs and pursued and killed the "famous horse-killing grizzly."

I have not heard of an authentic instance of a grizzly's eating human flesh. Numbers of hunters have been killed by grizzlies, but their bodies were not eaten; they were not killed for food. Many persons have lost their lives from storms, accidents, and starvation; yet their bodies have lain for days and weeks in territory frequented by grizzlies without being eaten by them. A prospector, his horse, and his burro were killed by a falling tree. Grizzlies devoured the bodies of the animals, but that of the prospector was not disturbed. Human flesh appears to be the only thing a grizzly does not eat.

The Long Winter Sleep

WHEN the food of the grizzly bear becomes scarce, he goes to bed and sleeps until a reasonable supply is available, even though he waits five months for it. He feasts on the fullness of the land during the summer and wraps himself in a thick blanket of fat. When winter comes on, he digs a hole and crawls in. This layer of fat is a non-conductor of cold and in due time is drawn on for food.

One autumn day I visited the Hallett Glacier with a professor from the University of Chicago. After exploring one of the upper crevasses, we stood looking down the steep slope of the glacier. New snow had fallen a few days before, and a soft, slushy coating still overlaid the ice. The professor challenged me to coast down the steep, snow-lubricated ice-slope. We seated ourselves on this soft, slippery snow, and he gave the word "Go." Just as we slid away, we saw at the bottom of the slope, where we were soon to be, a huge grizzly bear. I wish you might have seen our efforts as we tried to change our minds on that steep slope! The grizzly was busily eating grasshoppers, but he heard us coming and fled at a racing gallop, giving an excellent exhibition of his clumsy hind legs reaching out flat-footed.

Each autumn numbers of insects and sometimes bushels of grasshoppers either are blown upon the ice and snow or else approach it too closely and fall from having their wings chilled. Evidently the grizzlies long ago learned of this food-supply, for the ice-fields are regularly visited by them during the autumn. Along the timber-line the grizzly feeds freely upon the last of autumn's berries and the last green plants. Many a grizzly goes to the heights to put on fat for his long winter's sleep.

Bear food becomes scarce as winter approaches. Fruit, berries, grass, and weeds are out of season; most birds and insects are gone. The bear feeds on what remains—small animals which he digs out, a stray stranded fish, now and then a dead bird or animal carcass, the red fruit of the rose, and the nuts, bark, and roots of trees and plants. I do not believe the grizzly eats a special or a purgative food during the few days preceding his denning up, although he may do so.

On the few occasions when I have been able to keep track of a bear during the four or five days immediately preceding his retirement, he did not eat a single thing. I have examined a number of grizzlies that were killed while hibernating, and in every instance the stomach and intestines were empty. These facts lead me to conclude that bears rest and fast for a few days before going permanently to the winter den.

The bear generally prepares his winter quarters in advance of the time needed. He may occasionally sleep in his den before taking possession of it for the winter. But this is exceptional. In two cases that I know of he lay outside the den, though near it; and a number of other times he kept away from the den until he entered it for the long sleep. After the den is completely ready, the grizzly continues his usual search for food. Generally this requires long excursions and he may wander miles from the den.

In climbing along the bottom of a deep, narrow ravine one November day, I saw on the slope above me what appeared to be a carload or more of freshly dumped earth. My first thought was that a prospector was at work driving a tunnel; but upon examination it proved to be a recently finished but not yet occupied hibernating-den. The entrance was about three feet in diameter. Just inside the den was a trifle larger. It extended, nearly level, about twelve feet into the mountain-side. At the back it was six feet across and four feet high.

The size of the den varies and is apparently determined by the character of the soil in which it is made and also by the inclination of the bear making it. Most other dens measured were smaller than this one.

The grizzly may use the same den for several winters or have a new one each year. He may dig the den himself or take an old one that some other bear has used, or he may make use of one shaped by Nature—a cave or a rock-slide. I knew of one grizzly hibernating in a prospector's abandoned tunnel. Sometimes, like the black bear, he will dig a den on a steep mountain-side beneath the widely spreading roots of trees; sometimes beneath a large fallen log, close to the upturned roots which support it. In crossing the mountains one February I noticed a steamy vapor rising from a hole in the snow by the protruding roots of an overturned tree. I walked to the hole to investigate. The vapor was rank with the odor of a bear. Near my home on the slope of Long's Peak I have known grizzlies to den up beneath the snow-crushed, matted tree-growths at the timber-line, at an altitude of about eleven thousand feet.

Twice I have known bears to hibernate in enormous nests that were made of the long fibres of cedar bark. It must have taken days to construct

one of these nests, as more than forty cedar trees
had been more or less disrobed to supply material
for it. It resembled the nests of trash that razor-
back hogs in the South construct, though much
larger. The bear, after piling it up, worked his way
in near the bottom, somewhat after the fashion of a
boy crawling into a haycock. Over this hibernat-
ing-nest the snow spread its blanket and probably
afforded all the protection needed.

Sometimes the entrance to a den is partly closed
by the occupant. Once in, he reaches out and
claws the lower part full of earth, or rakes in trash
and leaves. In most instances nothing is done to
close the entrance. The snows drift back into the
den, pile upward, and at last close the entrance
most effectually.

All the dens that I recall were upon northerly or
easterly—the cooler—slopes. The snow as it fell
would be likely to remain and close or blanket the
entrance all winter long. Snow evidently enters
into the grizzly's winter plans.

Late one cold, snowless December I came upon a
grizzly carrying spruce boughs into his den. Evidently he had used the den and found it cold. The
den had a large opening; this he may have been
intending to close. The rocky floor was already
piled a foot deep with boughs. I have seen two
other dens with floor-coverings; one of these was of
pine twigs, and the other of coarse grass and
kinni-kinnick. But in most cases the bear sleeps
upon the uncovered rocks or the naked earth.

Snow is a factor in determining when a bear be-
gins his winter sleep. If he is fat and food is scarce,
an early, heavy snow is pretty certain to cause him
to turn in early. If no snow comes and food is still

to be had, the bear is likely to delay his hibernation.

The individual inclination of the bear and his condition—whether fat or thin—are also factors which influence his time of retiring. I knew of two bears, apparently of similar condition, one of whom turned in three weeks earlier than the other. Two bears whom I noticed one winter ran about more than a month after all the other bears had disappeared. Both were thin—just why I should like to know. They also turned in shortly after they became rounded out. Generally bears of a locality turn in for winter at about the same time. Hibernating may begin early in November, but in most localities, and in most years, the time is likely to be a month later.

In Alaska and the Northwest many bears hibernate in the heights above the timber-line. I have found a number in the mountains of Colorado with winter quarters at an altitude of twelve thousand feet. In southern Colorado and in the Yellowstone Park region many have denned up at about the altitude of six thousand feet. But a grizzly may hibernate anywhere in his territory where he can find or make a den to his liking.

Except when there are cubs, a grizzly dens alone. Accounts which tell of a number of full-grown grizzlies spending the winter in one den lack verification. The cubs are born in the hibernating-den, and they den up with the mother the first, and sometimes the second, winter after their birth. The cubs generally den up together the first winter after they are weaned.

Once in for the winter, the bear is likely to stay in the den for weeks. Most of the time probably is spent sleeping, and, so far as known, without either food or water. A bear may be routed out of his winter quarters without difficulty. Generally his sleep is not heavy enough greatly to deaden his senses. Hunters, trappers, floods, and snow-slides have driven grizzlies from their dens during every stage of hibernation, and in each case a moment after the bear came forth his senses were as alert as ever; he was able either to run away or to fight in his normal manner.

Prospectors in Jefferson Valley, Montana, told me of staking claims and starting to drive a tunnel early one December. A day or two after they began blasting they saw a bear break out of a snowy den and scamper away on the mountain-side. They tracked him to the place where he had holed up again. It was their belief that the noise or the jar of their shots had awakened and re-awakened the bear, until, disgusted, he left the region for a quieter sleeping-place.

A sniffling and grunting attracted my attention one midwinter day as I was snowshoeing along the side of a ravine. Presently, a short distance ahead of me, I saw a grizzly's nose thrust out of a hole in the snowy slope. Then his head followed. Sleepily the grizzly half-opened his eyes, then closed them again. His shaking and drooping head fell lower and lower, until with a jerk he raised it only to let it droop again. He repeated this performance a number of times. Evidently it was the head of a very sleepy grizzly. Occasionally he opened his eyes for a moment, but he did not seem interested in the outside world and he finally withdrew his head and disappeared in the den.

After midwinter, and especially towards spring, a bear sometimes comes out for fresh air and exercise, or to sun himself. One gray February day, snowshoeing along the Big South Poudre, I chanced to look across an opening from the edge of the woods and saw a grizzly walking round and round in a well-beaten pathway in the snow. Occasionally he reared up, faced about, and walked round in the opposite direction. His den was near by. Half a mile farther on I came upon a bear trail near the entrance to another den. Here the bear had walked back and forth in a pathway that was about sixty feet long. It was beaten down in the snow to a depth of fifteen inches. Two places showed that the bear had rolled and wallowed about in the snow.

Elsewhere, another year, about the middle of March, I examined much-worn pathways near a grizzly's den. These had been made at least three weeks before and had been used a number of times. One pathway led to the base of a cliff that faced the east, where the bear had probably lain in the morning sun. Another led to a much-used spot that caught the afternoon sun.

Perhaps a bear sometimes becomes tired or restless during his long winter sleep. Now and then he comes forth in spring with the fur worn off his hips, back, or shoulders. He may kill time, when through sleeping, with a short excursion outside the den. If the den is large, he sometimes tramples about like a caged animal.

Climatic conditions, the altitude at which the bear hibernated, and other factors determine the time when grizzlies leave their dens. Most of them come forth during March, but stragglers may not appear until late in April. Mothers with cubs remain in the den a few weeks longer than bears without cubs.

At the limits of tree growth, one cold March day,

I came upon the tracks of a grizzly bear descending the mountain. I back-tracked them and found the den in which the grizzly had spent the winter. The inside of the den was gravelly and comparatively clean. Only this single line of tracks led from the den, though the weather had been clear for a week; so I judged this was the first time the grizzly had sauntered forth. It was just sundown when I reached the den. The heights were icy, and I hesitated about continuing across the Divide that night, so concluded to occupy the den. I knew that bears often take a short ramble in the spring and then return to the den, but I took the chances of sharing it with him. I do not know what the grizzly did that night—whether or not he came back. But my fire in the mouth of the den may have kept him at bay.

The hard, cracked skin on the soles of the grizzly's feet is shed during hibernation, and the feet in spring are soft and tender. For several days he avoids traveling over rough places. His claws grow out during the winter rest, also. When he goes to sleep they are worn, broken, and blunt; but he comes out of winter quarters with claws long and moderately pointed.

What is the grizzly's condition in the spring after months of fasting? He has hibernated from three to five months, and in this time probably has taken neither water nor food. First of all he comes forth fat and not in the least hungry. The walls of his stomach have greatly contracted, almost completely closing the interior. Two stomachs which I saw taken from grizzlies killed early in the spring were as hard as chunks of rubber, and had capacity for not more than two or three spoonfuls. But when the grizzly reappears after his long winter sleep he is as strong as ever and can run for hours or fight with normal effectiveness.

He may not eat anything for a few days after leaving the den. For many days he eats lightly, and it may be two weeks before he has a normal appetite. His first food is likely to be the early, tender shoots of plants or trees, tuberous roots, swelling buds, and green grass.

I once watched a grizzly for seven days after he emerged from his hibernating-cave. His winter quarters were near timber-line on Battle Mountain, at an altitude of nearly twelve thousand feet. The winter had been of average temperature, but with scanty snow-fall. I saw him, by chance, just as he left the den, on the first day of March. He walked about aimlessly for an hour or more, then returned to his sleeping-place without eating or drinking anything.

The following day he wandered about until afternoon before he broke his fast. He ate a mouthful of willow twigs and took a taste of water. He walked leisurely down the mountain and towards sundown made himself a nest at the foot of a cliff in the woods. Here he remained, apparently sleeping, until late the next afternoon. Then, just before sundown, he walked out a short distance, smelled of a number of things, licked the snow a few times, and returned to his nest.

The fourth day he went early for water and ate more willow twigs. In the afternoon he came upon a dead bird—apparently a junco—which he ate. After another drink he lay down at the foot of a tree for the night. The following morning he drank freely of water, surprised and devoured a rabbit, and then lay down. He slept until noon the next day, then set out foraging; he found a dead mouse and toward evening caught another rabbit. The seventh day was much like the preceding one. During the first week out the grizzly did not eat food enough to make him one ordinary meal.

Hibernation is not well understood. The habit probably originated from the scarcity of food. However, in Mexico grizzlies sometimes hibernate even though the climate be mild and food plentiful. As these grizzlies probably came from the cold north, the habit may have been fixed in the species when it arrived. Hibernation appears to be helpful and not harmful, and it may therefore continue for ages even though not required. The rest which hibernation gives to mind and stomach, with the entire organism relaxed, may both increase efficiency and lengthen life.

The polar bear has its own peculiar hibernating-habits. The food of this bear is sea food. This is available even in the winter-time, on or beneath the ice. The male polar bears do not hibernate; the females do not except when about to give birth to young. The cubs at birth are small and helpless, and require the mother's constant care and the shelter of the den for some weeks after birth.

Mr. J. D. Figgins has written one of the best comments on hibernation that I have read. I quote as follows:

"The period of hibernation in any mammal not only varies in a given species, but is largely influenced by the available supply of food to which it is accustomed or that is necessary for its requirements.

"Examples of this character may be cited among several species of mammals. It is the custom of the chipmunks, or 'ground squirrels,' to hoard up at least a partial supply of food in the autumn for consumption during the winter months; but this is rarely, if ever, sufficient to keep these interesting little animals active for the entire period. In most localities, there is no available food with which to augment their scant store and they are never in evidence from late October to April. In other locations where the fruit of the Cratægus, or 'thorn apple,' is to be had, they may be seen almost daily, although the ground may be covered with several feet of snow and low temperatures prevail.

"Another example is the opossum. Ordinarily these animals are active throughout the entire year, but towards the northern edge of their range they frequently hibernate for considerable periods (thirty-one days from personal observations).

"Certain of the small rodents can, and probably do, hoard sufficient food for actual need during the winter months; but the problem is in direct ratio to the size of the animal. Hence we find the marmot, a much larger animal, making no provision, although his habitat is confined to the higher altitudes and his period of hibernation is extended over a greater length of time than many other species. His food consists wholly of grass and other green plants, and it is doubtful if he could subsist on dry food. Granting that he could, the amount required would be prohibitive, otherwise he would make some effort in that direction, as do the conies, a much smaller animal.

"Being omnivorous and of great size, a bear could not secure or preserve the necessary amount of food to carry him through five months. Such food could not consist of any variety other than vegetation, and he is not a 'hay' eater, and so, nature has provided him a means of surviving the long period of fasting and probably, without discomfort.

"It is well known that bears show a distinct preference for fruit during the late summer and autumn months. Not because that is the season for the various fruits, but through a need of their sugar content and its fattening qualities. Composed largely of juices which are quickly absorbed, the digestive process is very brief and the discarded residue is discharged at once. This may give rise to the belief that a purgative has been employed as a means of cleansing the bowels and explains the presence of unbroken berries in the excrement and the absence of offensive odors. As a means of exploding the purgative theory we need only refer to bears in captivity. Although the latter may be confined to cement floors and have no access to any matter whatever, other than the food regularly supplied, they frequently hibernate in a quite orderly manner.

"It must be conceded that bears are irregular in the period of 'holing up' and that they do so only when food has become too scarce to sustain activities without a drain upon the store of fat they have acquired; or during very severe weather. In the mean time there has been a gradual reduction in food as the period of hibernation approaches and a consequent lessened activity of the bowels. Nor is there reason for surprise because of the absence of excrement in the burrow and the presence of matter in the rectum when the bear emerges in the spring.

"In captivity bears may, or may not, hibernate. As a rule they 'sleep' for more or less varying periods during severe weather. One authority states the grizzly has been known to sleep from sixty to seventy-five days and during that time it was not difficult to awaken him. Black bears frequently pass the winter without evidence of even drowsiness. Others awake at irregular intervals, and after feeding lightly, return to their slumber."

The winter life of many animals is stern and strange. During the autumn the beaver stores up a food-supply for use when the pond is closed over with ice. The cony harvests hay for his winter food. Numbers of animals hunt food each day in the snow. But the woodchuck and the bear hibernate, that is, they fast and sleep in a den during the winter.

Being Good to Bears

ON the slope of Long's Peak one June morning I came upon two tiny grizzly bear cubs. Each was about the size of a cottontail rabbit—a lively little ball of fur, dark gray, almost black, in color.

Knowing that their mother had recently been killed, I thought I would capture them and bring them up properly. But they did not want to be brought up properly! We had a lively chase, dodging among the boulders and trees. Cornering them at last among the fallen logs, I grabbed one. He did the same to me. His teeth were as sharp as needles and almost as sharp were his lively claws. It was some time before I could tear myself loose. He kept a mouthful of my trousers. At last I deposited the fighting little fellow in the bottom of a sack. The other cub scratched and chewed me up and tore my clothes; but I forced it also into the sack. Two grizzly bears in the same sack! any one should have known better!

I started to conduct them personally to my cabin, two miles away. In descending a steep moraine with the sack over my shoulder I slipped and shook the sack more than any sack should have been shaken that contained two bears. Of course, they started to fight. One bit through the sack and bit the wrong bear. I finally reached my cabin with a long pole over my shoulder. Tied to the south end of the pole was a sack full of grizzly bears.

I shook the cubs out of the sack in front of a basin of milk and thrust their faces deeply into it.

Not having eaten for three days, they were "as hungry as bears" and needed no explanation concerning the milk. They had eager, cunning little faces, and were pets before sundown. In twenty-four hours Jenny knew that her name was Jenny, and Johnny that his was Johnny. After a few days they followed me about with fondness and loyalty.

These bears responded to kind treatment and were of cheerful disposition. I made it a point never to annoy or tease them. The grizzly bear is an exceedingly sensitive animal, and annoyances or cruelty make him cross. Once in addressing an audience concerning wild life I made the statement that bears would be good to us if we were good to them. A small boy instantly asked, "What do you do to be good to bears?" The health and the temper of bears, as well as of people, are easily ruined by improper food.

Young bear cubs are the most wide-awake and observing little people that I know of. Never have I seen a horse or dog who understood as readily or learned as rapidly as these two bears. One day I offered Johnny a saucer of milk. He was impatient to get it. Reaching up, he succeeded in spilling it, but he licked the saucer with satisfaction. On the second try he spilled only a part of the milk. On the third trial he clasped the saucer deftly in his two fore paws, lifted it upwards, turned his head back and poured the milk into his mouth.

When Johnny and Jenny were growing up, it seemed as if nothing unusual escaped them. A bright button, a flash of a ring, a white handkerchief, or an unusual movement or sound instantly caught their attention. They concentrated on each new object and endeavored to find out what it was. Having satisfied their curiosity or obtained full information about it, the next instant they were ready to concentrate on something else. But they remembered on second appearance anything which had especially interested them at any time. They learned through careful observation.

For a time they were not chained and had the freedom of the yard. Never have I seen two young animals more intense, more playful, or more energetic. They played alone, they mauled each other by the hour, and occasionally they scrapped. Sometimes we ran foot-races. From a scratch upon the ground, at the word "go," we would race down hill about one hundred and fifty yards. They were eager for these races and always ready to line up with me. They were so speedy that in every race they merrily turned around at least twice to see if I was coming, and in those days I was not slow.

Johnny and Jenny enjoyed playing with people, with any one who did not annoy them. Among the strangers who came was a man who made friends at once and had a good romp. When he left them and went to lunch, Johnny and Jenny followed and lay down near the door where he had disappeared. As he came out, they rose up and started another romp.

To attract my attention or to ask for something to eat, Johnny and Jenny would stand on hind legs and hold out fore paws like an orator. If I came around the corner of the house a quarter of a mile away, they instantly stood on tiptoe and gesticulated with enthusiasm. They were the life of my home, and occasionally almost the death of it.

It was almost impossible to get these cubs filled up. They ate everything—scraps from the table, rhubarb, dandelions, bitter sage, and bark—but they were especially fond of apples. If I approached with meat and honey upon a plate but with apples or turnips in my pockets, they would ignore the plate and, clinching me, thrust their noses into my pockets to find the promised treat.

One August evening I brought in a cluster of wild raspberries for Johnny and Jenny. While still more than a hundred feet from the cabin, both bears leaped to their feet, scented the air, and came racing to meet me with more than their ordinary enthusiasm. No child of frontier parents could have shown more interest in a candy package on the father's return from the city than did Johnny and Jenny in those berries.

A number of people were waiting in my cabin to see me. The little bears and I crowded in. I handed Jenny a berry-laden spray, and then one to Johnny, alternating until they were equally divided. Standing erect, each held the cluster under the left forearm by pressing it against the chest. When browsing in a raspberry-patch bears commonly bite off the tips of the canes together with the leaves and the berries. Johnny and Jenny ate more daintily. One berry was plucked off at a time with two front claws and dropped into the mouth. As one berry followed another, the lips were smacked, and the face and every movement made expressed immense satisfaction at the taste.

Every one crowded close to watch the performance. In the jostling one of the berry-laden canes fell to the floor. Both little bears grabbed for it at the same instant. They butted heads, lost their temper, and began to fight over it. I grabbed them by the collars and shook them.

"Why, Johnny and Jenny," I said, "why do you do this? And such awful manners when we have company! What shall I do with you?"

They instantly stopped quarreling and even forgot the berries. For several seconds the little bears were embarrassed beyond all measure. They simply stared at the floor. Then suddenly each appeared to have the same idea. Standing erect, facing each other, they put fore paws on each other's shoulders, and went "Ungh, ah, oooo." Plainly they were very sorry that they had misbehaved.

The manner in which these cubs received the berries, the fact that the first time they saw mushrooms they scented them at some distance and raced for them, also that on other occasions they went out of their way to get a plant ordinarily liked by the grizzly, led me to think that they inherited a taste for a number of things that grizzlies commonly eat.

One day we were out walking, when we came upon an army of ants. Without the least hesitation Johnny and Jenny followed along the line, licking them up. Upon reaching the stone behind which the ants were disappearing, Johnny thrust one fore claw under it and flung it aside. I was astonished at his strength.

I tried not to teach Johnny or Jenny any trick, but encouraged them to develop any original stunt or individuality of their own. One day Jenny was attracted by a big green fly that alighted on Johnny. She struck at it; the fly relighted and she struck again. With a little effort I succeeded in getting the bears to shoo flies off each other, and sometimes they were both busy at the same time. It made a comical show, especially when one was lazily lying down and the other was shooing with eagerness and solemnity.

Another activity I encouraged was the bear's habit of holding the other around the neck with one fore paw and rubbing or scratching the back of the bear's head with his other paw. In a short time both bears, while facing each other, would go through the performance at the same time.

Like other children Johnny and Jenny were fond of water and spent much time rolling and wading in the brook by their shed. This was a play they enjoyed. I showed interest in having them roll and splash in the liveliest manner possible.

Johnny seemed unusually interested in what I was doing one day and imitated in succession a number of my performances. I had dropped a penny on the floor, and then, stooping over, touched it with the end of one finger and moved it rapidly about. He rose on his hind feet, held up one claw, then, stooping, put this upon the penny and moved it rapidly about. Blowing the yolk out of an egg, I held up the empty shell before him, and then proceeded to move it rapidly about on the floor with the point of one finger. After licking the shell Johnny imitated my every act without crushing the shell.

While Jenny was asleep on the grass, I placed a large umbrella over her. When she opened her eyes, she at once commenced a quiet though frightened study of the strange thing. She closed one eye, turned her head to one side, and looked up into it; then, turning her head, closed the other eye for a look. A sudden puff of wind gave life to the umbrella and this in turn to Jenny. She made a desperate dash to escape the mysterious monster. The wind whirled the umbrella before her and she landed in it. Wrecking the umbrella, she fled in terror, bellowing with every jump. It took more than an hour to explain matters and assure Jenny that I had not been playing any tricks.

Scotch, my short-nosed collie, was with me when Johnny and Jenny were growing up. Johnny and Scotch were fond of each other, and though each was a little jealous of the master's attention to the other, they got along admirably. Ofttimes they wrestled, and sometimes in their rough and tumble they played pretty roughly. As a climax often Scotch would aim for a neck-hold on Johnny and hammer him on the tip of his sensitive nose with one fore paw, while Johnny if possible would seize Scotch's tail in his mouth and shut down on it with his needle-like teeth.

One of the most interesting pranks which they played on each other was over a bone. Scotch was enjoying this, when he discovered Johnny watching him eagerly. Plainly Johnny wanted that bone. After a little while Scotch leaped to his feet, looked off in the direction beyond Johnny and barked, as though some object of interest was coming from that direction. Then, picking up the bone, he walked away. As he passed in front of Johnny he dropped the bone and gave a bark. Going on a short distance, he barked once or twice more and lay down watching this pretended object in the distance. Johnny was more interested in the bone, but Scotch had dropped this a foot or two beyond his reach, chained as he was. For some time Johnny stood with his nose pointing at the bone, apparently thinking deeply as to how he might reach it. At last, stretching his chain to the utmost he reached out with his right arm. But he could not touch it. Although realizing that he probably could not reach it with the left arm, nevertheless he tried.

All this time Scotch was watching Johnny out of the corner of his eye and plainly enjoyed his failures. Johnny stood looking at the bone; Scotch continued looking at Johnny. Suddenly Johnny had an idea. He wheeled about, reached back with his hind foot and knocked the bone forward where he could pick it up with fore paws. Scotch, astonished, leaped to his feet and walked off without a bark or once looking back.

When Johnny and Jenny were small they often reminded me of a little boy and a little girl. Ofttimes they would follow me into my cabin. If I sat down they would come close, stand on hind legs, put fore paws on my knees, and look up at me. They would play with my watch-string, peep into my pockets, notice my pencil, or look at the buttons on my coat. Sometimes they would make a round of the room, scrutinize an unusual knot in a log, or stop to look for several seconds at the books in the shelves or the last magazine-cover. Then again, like children, they would walk round the room, tap with their fore paws here and there, and hurry on as children do. More than once they climbed up into my lap, twitched my ears, touched my nose, played with my hair, and finally fell off to sleep, one on each arm.

One day, while I was carrying Johnny in my arms, it occurred to me that he would enjoy a big rocking-chair. I placed him in a chair with one fore paw on each arm. He sat up like a little old man. As I started the chair rocking, he showed his suspicion and alarm by excitedly peering over, first at one rocker and then the other. Presently he calmed down and seemed to enjoy the movement. By and by he caught the swing and rocked himself. Suddenly the little old man and the rocker went over backward. Seeing his angry look as he struck the floor, I leaped upon the centre table. Getting on his feet, he struck a blow that barely missed me and then made lively bites at my ankles. He blamed me for the law of falling bodies. After a few seconds he was as playful as ever, remembering that I had never played any tricks on him, and realizing that I was not to blame for what had happened.

These little bears grew rapidly. At the age of seven months Johnny weighed approximately sixty pounds, and Jenny forty-six.

Numerous visitors and the increasing size of the cubs at last compelled me to chain them. The little bears were almost always on the move, either pacing back and forth or circling. Their long chains often got tangled with sticks, grass, or bushes. Sometimes the cubs showed impatience, but usually they carefully examined the chain, then, taking it in their fore paws, stepped this way and that and generally made the very move needed to extricate or unwind it. While doing this they appeared almost comical because of their serious and concentrated attention.

One morning Johnny climbed to the top of the pole fence to which he was chained. With happy, playful activity he galloped atop the pole to the end of the chain; then, like an engine, he reversed his direction without turning and went hippety-hop back again. This was a favorite exercise of Johnny's, a game which I had encouraged; but this morning while having a beautiful time he tumbled off backward. The chain caught in a knot and Johnny found himself hung. Grizzly bears resent being hung by the neck. Johnny quickly kicked himself out of his collar. Finding himself free, and thinking himself abused, I suppose, he ran away. After three days this runaway boy concluded to come home. I saw him come out of the woods into an opening on the mountain-side. Even at a distance I could see that he no longer possessed the big round stomach that he took away. I went to meet him. He was interested in the food question, and long before he reached me he was dancing about with outstretched arms.

In the midst of this performance it occurred to him that if he wanted anything to eat he must hurry to me. So he checked his first impulse and started to carry his second into instant effect. These incomplete proceedings interrupted and tripped each other three or four times and mixed themselves together. Apparently an entangled mental process followed my appearance. Though he tumbled about in comic confusion while trying to do two things at once, it was evident through it all that his central idea was to get something to eat.

One September we went camping out in Wild Basin, Johnny and Jenny racing along as happy as two boys. Sometimes they were ahead of me, sometimes behind; occasionally they stopped to wrestle and box. At night they lay close to me beside the camp-fire. Often I used one of them for a pillow, and more than once I awoke to find that they were using me for one.

As we were climbing along the top of a moraine, a black bear and her two cubs came within perhaps thirty feet of us. They saw or scented us. The cubs and their mother bristled up and ran off terribly frightened, while Johnny and Jenny only a short distance in front of me, walked on, both ludicrously pretending that they had not seen the black bears. Surely they were touched with aristocracy!

The man in charge of my place neither understood nor sympathized with wide-awake and aggressive young grizzlies, and once, when I was away, he teased Johnny. The inevitable crash came and the man went to the hospital. On another occasion he set a pan of sour milk on the ground before Jenny. Bears learn to like sour milk, but Jenny had not learned and she sourly sniffed at it. The man roared, "Drink it," and kicked her in the ribs. Again we had to send for the ambulance.

At last it appeared best to send Johnny and Jenny to the Denver Zoo. Two years went by before I allowed myself the pleasure of visiting them. A number of other bears were with them in a large pen when I leaped in, calling "Hello, Johnny!" as I did so. Johnny jumped up fully awake, stood erect, extended both arms, and gave a few joyful grunts in the way of greeting. Back among the other bears stood Jenny on tiptoe, eagerly looking on.

Trailing Without a Gun

I HAD gone into Wild Basin, hoping to see and to trail a grizzly. It was early November and the sun shone brightly on four inches of newly fallen snow; trailing conditions were excellent. If possible I wanted to get close to a bear and watch his ways for a day or two.

Just as I climbed above the last trees on the eastern slope of the Continental Divide, I saw a grizzly ambling along the other side of a narrow canyon, boldly outlined against the sky-line. I was so near that with my field-glasses I recognized him as "Old Timberline," a bear with two right front toes missing. He was a silver-tip—a nearly white old bear. For three days I followed Old Timberline through his home territory and camped on his trail at night. I had with me hatchet, kodak, field-glasses, and a package of food, but no gun.

The grizzly had disappeared by the time I crossed the canyon, but a clear line of tracks led westward. I followed them over the Divide and down into the woods on the other side. In a scattered tree-growth the tracks turned abruptly to the right, then led back eastward, close to the first line of tracks, as though Old Timberline had turned to meet any one who might be following him.

The most impressive thing I had early learned in trailing and studying the grizzly was that a wounded bear if trailed and harassed will sometimes conceal himself and lie in an ambush in wait for his pursuer. I never took a chance of walking into such danger. Whenever the trail passed a log, boulder, or bushes that might conceal a bear, I turned aside and scouted the ambush for a side view before advancing further.

Old Timberline's tracks showed that he had now and then risen on hind feet, listened and turned to look back. He acted as though he knew I was following him, but this he had not yet discovered. All grizzlies are scouts of the first order; they are ever on guard. When at rest their senses do continuous sentinel duty, and when traveling they act exactly as though they believed some man was in pursuit.

Following along the trail and wondering what turn the grizzly would make next, I found where he had climbed upon a ledge in the edge of an opening, and had evidently stood for some seconds, looking and listening. From the ledge he had faced about and continued his course westward, heading for a spur on the summit of the Divide.

We were in what is now the southern end of the Rocky Mountain National Park. The big bear and myself were on one of the high sky-lines of the earth. We traversed a territory ten thousand to twelve thousand feet above sea-level, much of it above the limits of tree growth. There were long stretches of moorland, an occasional peak towering above us, and ridges long and short thrusting east and west, and canyons of varying width and depth were to be seen below us from the summit heights.

Crossing this spur of the Divide, the grizzly entered the woods. Here he spent so much time rolling logs about and tearing them open for grubs and ants that I nearly caught up with him. I watched him through the scattered trees from a rocky ledge until he moved on. This after a few minutes he did. As he came to an opening in the woods, I wondered whether he would go round it to the right or to the left. To my astonishment, without the least hesitation he sauntered across the opening, his head held low and swinging easily from side to side. But the instant he was screened by trees beyond, rising up, with fore paws resting against a tree, he peered cautiously out to see if he was being followed. When the next opening in the woods was reached, he went discreetly round it. You never know what a grizzly's next move will be nor how to anticipate his actions.

Old Timberline started down into a canyon as though to descend a gully diagonally to the bottom. I hastily made a short cut and was ready to take his picture when he should come out at the lower end. But he never came. After waiting some time, I back-tracked and found he had gone only a few hundred feet down the gully, then returned to the top of the canyon and followed along the rim for a mile. He had then descended directly to the bottom of the canyon and gone straight up to the top on the other side.

Autumn is the time when bears most search the heights for food. Old Timberline's trail headed again for the heights. When I next caught sight of him, he was digging above the tree-line, but as it was now nearly night, I went back a short distance into the woods and built a fire by the base of a cliff. Here all through the clear night I had a glorious view of the high peaks up among the cold stars.

Before daylight I left camp and climbed to the top of a treeless ridge, thinking that the bear might come along that way. In the course of time he appeared, about a quarter of a mile east of me. After standing and looking about for a few minutes, he started along the ridge, evidently planning to re-cross the Continental Divide near where he had crossed the day before. As I could not get close to him from this point, I concluded to follow his trail of the preceding night and if possible find out what he had been doing.

A short distance below him I found his trail and back-tracked to a place which showed that he had spent the night near the entrance of a recently dug den. I learned some weeks later that this den was where he hibernated that winter. A short distance farther on I came to where he had been digging when I saw him the evening before. Evidently he had been successful. A few drops of blood on the snow showed that he had captured some small animal, probably a cony. From this point I trailed Old Timberline forward and eastward, and near noon I caught a glimpse of him on the summit of the Divide.

While roaming above timber-line he did not take the precaution to travel with his face in the wind. He could see toward every point of the compass. He was ambling easily along, but I knew that his senses were wide awake—that his sentinel nose never slept and that his ears never ceased to hear. Climbing to the very summit of a snow-covered ridge, he lay down with his back to the wind. Evidently he depended upon the wind to carry the warning scent of any danger behind him, while he was on the lookout for anything in front of him. Nothing could approach nearer than half a mile without his knowing it. He looked this way and that. After only a short rest he arose and started on again.

I hoped that some time I should be able to photograph Old Timberline at twenty-five or thirty feet. But at all times, too, I was more eager to watch him, to see what he was eating, where he went, and what he did. I was constantly trying to get as close as possible. Of course I had ever to keep in mind that he must not see, hear, nor scent me. I had to be particularly careful to prevent his scenting me. Often in hastening to reach a point of vantage I had to stop, note the topography, and change my direction, because a wind-current up an unsuspected canyon before me might carry news of my presence to the bear.

Near mountain-tops the wind is deflected this way and that by ridges and canyons. In a small area the prevailing west wind may be a north wind, and a short distance farther on it may blow from the southwest. Often, when the bear was somewhere in a canyon, I climbed entirely out of it, to avoid the likelihood of being scented, and scurried ahead on a plateau.

Usually I followed in the bear's trail, but sometimes I made short cuts. So long as Old Timberline remained on the moorland summit of this treeless ridge, I could not get close to him. But when he arose and started down the ridge, I hurried down the slope, hoping to get ahead and hide in a place of concealment near which he might pass. I kept out of sight in the woods and hastened forward for two miles, then climbed up and hid in a rock-slide on the rim of the ridge.

By and by I saw Old Timberline coming. When within five hundred feet of me he stopped and dug energetically. Buckets of earth flew behind, and occasionally a huge stone was torn out and hurled with one paw to the right or left. Once he stopped digging, rose on hind feet, and looked all around as though he felt that some one was slipping up on him. He dug for a few minutes longer and then again stood up and sniffed the air. Not satisfied, he walked quickly to a ledge from which he could see down the slope to the woods. Discovering nothing suspicious, he returned to his digging, stepping in his former footprints. He uncovered something in its nest, and through my glasses I saw him strike right and left and then rush out in pursuit of it. After nosing about in the hole where he had been digging, he started off again. He went directly to the ledge, walking in his former well-tracked trail, then descended the steep eastern slope of the Divide toward the woods. I hurried to the ledge from which he had surveyed the surroundings and watched him.

Arriving at a steep incline on the snowy slope, Old Timberline sat down on his haunches and coasted. A grizzly bear coasting on the Continental Divide! How merrily he went, leaning forward with his paws on his knees! At one place he plunged over a snowy ledge and dropped four or five feet. He threw up both fore paws with sheer joy. Soon he found himself exceeding the speed-limit. Looking back over one shoulder, and reaching out his paw behind him, he put on brakes; but as this did not check him sufficiently, he whirled about and slid flat on his stomach, digging in with both fingers and toes until he slowed down.

Then, sitting up on his haunches again, he set himself in motion by pushing along with rapid backward strokes of both fore paws. He coasted on toward the bottom. In going down a steep pitch of one hundred feet or more he either quite lost control of himself or let go from sheer enthusiasm. He rolled, tumbled, and slid recklessly along. Reaching the bottom, he rose on hind feet, looked about him for a few seconds, and then climbed halfway up the course for another coast. At the end of this merry sliding he landed on an open flat in the edge of the woods.

As it was nearly dark and I should not be able to see or follow the bear much longer, I concluded to roll a rock from the ledge down near him. Twice I had noticed that he had paid no attention to rocks that broke loose above and rolled near him. But he heard this rock start and rose up to look at it. It stopped a few yards from him. He sniffed the air with nose pointing toward it and then went up and smelled it. Rearing up instantly, he looked intently toward the mountain-top where I was hidden. After two or three seconds of thought he turned and ran. Evidently the stone had carried my scent to him. It was useless to follow him in the night.

The next morning I left camp and followed Old Timberline's trail through the woods. He had run for nearly ten miles almost straight south until coming to a small stream. Then for some distance he concealed, involved, and confused his trail with a cleverness that I have never seen equaled. Most animals realize that they leave a scent which enables other animals to follow them, but the grizzly is the only animal that I know who appears to be fully aware that he is leaving telltale tracks. He will make unthought-of turns and doublings to walk where his tracks will not show, and also tramples about to leave a confusion of tracks where they do show.

Arriving at the stream, the bear crossed on a fallen log and from the end of this leaped into a bushy growth beyond. I made a détour, thinking to find his tracks on the other side of the bushes, and I threw stones into the bushes, not caring to go into them. Both tracks and grizzly seemed to have vanished. I went down stream just outside the bushes bordering it, expecting every instant to find the grizzly's tracks, but not finding them. Then I returned to the log on which he had crossed the stream, and from which he had leaped into the bushes.

Examining the tracks carefully, I now discovered what I had before overlooked. After leaping into the bushes the bear had faced about and leaped back to the log, stepping carefully into his former tracks. From the log he had entered the water and waded up stream for a quarter of a mile. Of course not a track showed. At a good place for concealing his trail he had leaped out of the water into a clump of willows on the north bank. From the willows he made another long leap into the snow and then started back northward, alongside his ten-mile trail and one hundred feet from it, as though intending to return to the place where I had rolled the stone down the slope near him.

I did not discover all this at once, however. In my search for his trail I went up stream on the north side and passed, without noticing, the crushed willows into which he had leaped. Crossing to where the bank was higher, I started back down stream on the other side, and in doing so chanced to look across and see the crushed clump of willows. But it took me hours to untangle this involved trail.

When I had followed the tracks northward for more than a mile, the trail vanished in a snowless place. Apparently the grizzly had planned in advance to use this bare place, because the moves he made in it were those most likely to bewilder the pursuer. He did three things which are always more or less confusing and even bewildering to the pursuer, be he man or dog. He changed his direction, he left no tracks, and he crossed his former trail, thereby mixing the scents of the two. He confused the nose, left no record for the eye, and broke the general direction.

Unable to determine the course the bear had taken across this trackless place, I walked round it, keeping all the time in the snow. When more than halfway round I came upon his tracks leaving the bare place. Here he had changed his direction of travel abruptly from north to east, crossed his former trail, gone on a few yards farther, and then abruptly changed from east to north.

I hurried along his tracks. After a few miles I saw where perhaps the night before he had eaten part of the carcass of a bighorn. To judge from tooth marks, the sheep had been killed by wolves. The trail continued in general northward, parallel to the summit and a little below it. As I followed, the tracks approached timber-line, the trees being scattered and the country quite open.

Suddenly the trail broke off to the right for five or six hundred feet into the woods, as though Old Timberline had remembered an acquaintance whom he must see again. He had hustled along straight for a much-clawed Engelmann spruce, a tree with bear-claw and tooth marks of many dates, though none were recent. Old Timberline, apparently, had smelled the base of the tree and then risen up and sniffed the bark as high as his nose could reach. He had neither bitten nor clawed. Then he had gone to two near-by trees, each of which had had chunks bitten or torn out, and here smelled about.

Retracing his tracks to where the trail had turned off abruptly, the bear resumed his general direction northward. When he stopped on a ridge and began digging, I hurried across a narrow neck of woods and crept up as close as I dared. A wagonload of dirt and stones had been piled up. While I watched the digging, a woodchuck rushed out, only to be overtaken and seized by the bear, who, having finished his meal, shuffled on out of sight.

I followed the trail through woods, groves, and openings. After an hour or more without seeing the grizzly, I climbed a cliff, hoping to get a glimpse of him on some ridge ahead. I could see his line of tracks crossing a low ridge beyond and felt that he might still be an hour or so in the lead. But, in descending from the cliff, I chanced to look back along my trail. Just at that moment the bear came out of the woods behind me. He was trailing me!

I do not know how he discovered that I was following him. He may have seen or scented me. Anyway, instead of coming directly back and thus exposing himself, he had very nearly carried out his well-planned surprise when I discovered him. I found out afterwards that he had left his trail far ahead, turning and walking back in his own footprints for a distance, and trampling this stretch a number of times, and that he had then leaped into scrubby timber and made off on the side where his tracks did not show in passing along the trampled trail. He had confused his trail where he started to circle back, so as not to be noticed, and slipped in around behind me.

But after discovering the grizzly on my trail I went slowly along as though I was unaware of his near presence, turning in screened places to look back. He followed within three hundred feet of me. When I stopped he stopped. He occasionally watched me from behind bushes, a tree, or a boulder. It gave me a strange feeling to have this big beast following and watching me so closely and cautiously. But I was not alarmed.

I concluded to turn tables on him. On crossing a ridge where I was out of sight, I turned to the right and ran for nearly a mile. Then, circling back into our old trail behind the bear, I traveled serenely along, imagining that he was far ahead. I was suddenly startled to see a movement of the grizzly's shadow from behind a boulder near the trail, only three hundred feet ahead. He was in ambush, waiting for me! At the place where I left the trail to circle behind him, he had stopped and evidently surmised my movements. Turning in his tracks, he had come a short distance back on the trail and lain down behind the boulder to wait for me.

I went on a few steps after discovering the grizzly, and he moved to keep out of sight. I edged toward a tall spruce, which I planned to climb if he charged, feeling safe in the knowledge that grizzlies cannot climb trees. Pausing by the spruce, I could see his silver-gray fur as he peered at me from behind the boulder, and as I moved farther away I heard him snapping his jaws and snarling as though in anger at being outwitted.

Just what he would have done had I walked into his ambush can only be guessed. Hunters trailing a wounded grizzly have been ambushed and killed. But this grizzly had not even been shot at nor harassed.

Generally, when a grizzly discovers that he is followed, or even if he only thinks himself followed, he at once hurries off to some other part of his territory, as this one did after I rolled the stone. But Old Timberline on finding himself followed slipped round to follow me. Often a grizzly, if he feels he is not yet seen—that his move is unsus-pected—will slip round to follow those who are trailing him. But in no other case that I know of has a bear lingered after he realized that he was seen. After Old Timberline discovered that I had circled behind him, he knew that I knew where he was and what he was doing.

But instead of running away he came back along the trail to await my coming. What were his inten-tions? Did he intend to assault me, or was he over-come with curiosity because of my unusual actions and trying to discover what they were all about? I do not know. I concluded it best not to follow him farther, nor did I wish to travel that night with this crafty, soft-footed fellow in the woods. Going a short distance down among the trees, I built a rousing fire. Between it and a cliff I spent the night, satisfied that I had had adventure enough for one outing.

Trailing is adventurous. Many of the best lessons of woodcraft that I have learned, several of the greatest and most beneficial outings that I have had, were those during which I followed, some-times day and night, that master of strategy, the grizzly bear. A few times in trailing the grizzly I have outwitted him, but more frequently he has outwitted me. Every grizzly has speed, skill, and endurance. He has mental capacity and often shows astounding plan, caution, courage, and audacity.

Trailing without a gun is red-blooded life, scouting of the most exacting and manly order. The trailer loses himself in his part in the primeval play of the wilderness. It is doubtful if any other experience is as educational as the trailing of the grizzly bear.

When the Grizzly Plays

ONE of the best play-exhibitions that I have ever enjoyed was that of a grizzly juggling with an eight-foot log in a mountain stream. In examining the glaciation of the Continental Divide, five or six miles west of Long's Peak, I came out of the woods into a little meadow by the East Inlet of Grand Lake, where I saw the grizzly and the log, rolling and tumbling in the water. The log bobbed and plunged about as the bear struggled with it in the swift current.

The big, shaggy grizzly, wild and gray, fitted into the wild mountain scene. A peak bristling with ledges and dotted with snow towered in the blue sky behind. Down the steep incline of the peak the clear, cold stream came with subdued roar, as it rushed the inclines and the rapids of its solid rock-cut channel. The opposite wall of the canyon was of glacier-polished granite, while behind me the wall rose steeply, covered with a crowded growth of towering spruce. It was a grand wilderness playground.

As I watched from the edge of the woods, the grizzly once hugged the log between fore paws, stood it on end in the water, and then tried to climb it. His weight caused it to tip him over. The log escaped from the bear and started to float away, but he was after it with a rush.

Another time he lay across it and splashed about like a boy on a pole trying to learn to swim. Getting too far forward, he rolled under the log. Struggling on his back, he grasped it between all four feet. Then he took it beneath one forearm and suddenly ducked it into deep water. It shot out into the middle of the stream with the bear splashing wildly in pursuit. At last he succeeded in securing a good hold with his teeth and was tugging the log toward the bank when he saw a stick floating down stream. As he turned to seize it, his wave pushed the stick farther away and at the same time gave the log a start down stream. Turning from the stick, he hurried to seize the log. Pushing it end on against the rocky bank, and pressing against it with one fore paw, he looked over his shoulder as though intending to seize the stick. But this was out of reach, hurrying down stream.

Next he appeared to be trying to walk the log. When he was almost on it, the log rolled and with a splash the grizzly fell into the water on his side. For a second he lost sight of the log, or pretended that he had, and took swift glances this way and that. As it bumped into his up-stream side, he seized it with feigned surprise. Then he took it to the bank in shallow water, mauling it about, biting and gnawing at it. As the log rolled from side to side, he swam around it, batting it and pushing it under.

A number of Clarke nutcrackers and magpies had collected and in astonishment watched the exhibition. Ordinarily a nutcracker is noisy in autumn, screaming and chuckling loudly and harshly. But these were motionless and silent as they watched. A passing magpie whirled aside to see the show, and was just alighting on the bank when the bear splashed water wildly with a sweeping stroke at the log. With confused haste the magpie retreated. Taking a stand on a solitary spruce which leaned over the bank, he watched the scene without a move. The other birds, equally intent, watched from a high-water log-jam among large near-by boulders.

At last the grizzly secured the log just under water. Standing upon it with hind feet, he reached down with both fore paws and went through an up-and-down motion like a washerwoman. Then he left the log and walked along the bank, keeping watch of it as it floated slowly down stream. It gradually pulled off from the bank. When it was about ten feet away he leaped playfully after it with feet outspread like those of a flying squirrel. Letting it drift again, he watched it intently as it was swept into the current and floated away in midstream. By swimming and wading he kept alongside for some distance, then put one fore paw upon it. Perhaps he was about to start something new, but just then he scented something over his right shoulder.

Releasing the log, he climbed upon a boulder that projected above the water. On hind feet, interested and curious, he stood gazing for some seconds. Evidently desiring more information, he started ashore and never looked back at the log hurrying away down the rapids.

I found afterwards that the grizzly had rolled the log into the water a short distance up stream from where I came upon him. The log was a sound section of a spruce that had broken off when the tree fell among boulders and lay on the bank a few feet from the water. The bear had come down stream, and in passing ten or twelve feet from the log had turned aside to it. He may have rolled it over to see if there were insects beneath, but, accidentally or intentionally, he had rolled it into the water.

This play of a grizzly with an object is much less common than their other play, such as coasting. Several times I have seen grizzlies lying on their stomachs sliding down a steep, smooth, grassy slope, or trying to start themselves on a slope that was not steep enough for coasting. A grizzly pauses to play frequently. A mother and cubs often play together in the water, with apparent enjoyment for all. Many a beaver pond is a favorite swimming-hole for the cubs and a wading-place for the older bears.

I watched an old grizzly romping in the mud of a shallow pond. After rolling and wallowing about, until his fur coat was covered with mud thick enough to form a plaster cast, he grew energetic. He ran for the shore with all speed, as though hunters and dogs were upon him. Once out of the mud, he turned and raced back through the pond, galloping all the way across and sending the mud and water flying in exciting fashion. After a momentary pause he again galloped through the mud and water to the other side. The pond was half filled with sediment, and evidently the mud was more than a foot deep.

One autumn while camping on the Continental Divide near the head of Forest Canyon, I discovered that a grizzly will sometimes climb a slope for the purpose of coasting. While I was watching a flock of bighorn sheep, a grizzly came to the summit of a near-by mountain. I saw him as he reached the top and supposed he was crossing to the other side. He shuffled along apparently with definite plans in mind. But he was not going over the top. He headed straight for an out-jutting ridge where the wind-blown snow from the summit had formed a cornice at the top of its steep snowy slope.

The Grizzly, "Our greatest wild animal."

Photos by Leonard Lee Rue, III

"In this sequence of photographs, a mother grizzly nuzzles her 16-ounce twins on their first day of life (above), and inspects a squalling cub while the other infant nurses (above right). In the third photo the tiny cubs, now 3 days old, nestle in the vast forest of their mother's fur (below right)."

Grizzly bear cub, two months old.

Full grown grizzly bear.

Grizzly bear cub, alert and curious at two months.

Photo by Henry Monroe

A growing cub, "this creature that walks like a man—the greatest animal without a voice."

Photo by W. J. Schoonmaker
"The most impressive animal on the continent."

The grizzly hurled himself headlong upon the snow cornice with fore paws outstretched. The cornice gave way beneath him. The snow slid and snow-dust whirled about him. I had glimpses of him looking like a fur-robed Eskimo falling down a snowy precipice in a blizzard. As the snow-dust cleared, it revealed the grizzly seated in a moving mass of snow, coasting swiftly down.

The snow went to pieces on a nearly hidden rock-point and spilled the coaster. He rolled, then slid, first on his stomach head first, then on his back feet first, but collected himself at the bottom. Rising and bearing away from the deep snow, he climbed up again and appeared to look with interest at the gully he had made in the slope as he coasted and also at the scattered marks where he was spilled.

Just beneath the cornice he waded into the snow. He shook himself, kicked the snow, went through swimming motions but still did not start to slide. The slope was not steep enough. Wallowing down a short distance, he rose, then rolled forward over and over—cartwheeled. After three or four turns he began to slide. This stirred up so much snow-dust that I could get only dim glimpses of him and could not tell whether he was sliding head first or tail first. On the thin snow at the bottom the dust-fog cleared, and the grizzly rolled over and over down the slope like a log. Getting on his feet, he walked away and disappeared behind the storm-battered trees at timber-line.

I took pains to track the bear. Down in the woods, more than three miles from his coasting-place, he had made a meal the evening before off the smelly old carcass of a deer. He spent the night by the bones. In the morning he climbed to the top of a ridge that rose above the tree-tops. His tracks showed that he had walked about here and stopped at three or four places to look down on scenes below.

Then he had followed his tracks back close to where he had spent the night. Here he had tramped about in the snow as though having nothing in particular to do. But a coyote was trying to find something on the bones and the bear may have been threatening him. He finally started off, plainly with coasting in his mind, for without stopping he went directly to the snow cornice. From tracks which I saw in this and other canyons I realized that a grizzly sometimes goes out of his way in order to coast down steep snowy places.

A grizzly that I was following one November morning was evidently well fed, for he traveled slowly along with apparently nothing to do. Descending the ridge on which he had been walking, he came upon the side of a steep southern slope, across the ravine from where I had paused to watch him. Occasionally a bush or weed sprang up as the warm sun released it from its little burden of snow. If it was close to him, he reached out one paw and stroked or boxed it daintily and playfully as a kitten; or, if a few feet away, he stopped, turned his head to one side, and looked at it with lazy, curious interest. He turned for a better glimpse of a tall willow springing up as if inviting him to play and appeared just ready to respond when he caught sight of his moving dark-blue shadow against the white slope. Instantly, reaching out lightly with one fore paw, he commenced to play with the shadow. As it dodged, he tried to reach it with the other paw, then stopped to look at it. He sat down and watched it intently, ready to strike it if it moved; he pushed his nose closer to it. Keeping his eyes on the shadow, with a sudden leap he threw both fore paws forward and brought them down where the shadow had been before his move. For several seconds he leaped and struck right and left in his vain efforts to catch it. Then, seated on his haunches, he watched the shadow out of one eye. He turned his head, possibly wondering what the shadow would do. He seemed surprised to find that it was not behind him, and turned back quickly to see where it was. Did the grizzly know what this shadow-thing was, and was all this just jolly make-believe? In any case, he was playing and playing merrily. When I first watched him he reminded me of a kitten, but the longer he played the more his actions resembled those of a puppy and finally those of dog.

As the grizzly backed slowly down the slope, he watched the shadow following him, and made a feint as though about to grab it, but stopped. Slowly he started after the shadow up the slope, then pursued it with a rush. Then, backing away along the side of the slope, he watched the shadow out of the corner of his eye. He suddenly stopped and stood as though thinking; then wheeled, faced down the slope, and looked off into the distance. After a second he slowly turned his head and looked over first one shoulder, then the other, for the shadow. Finally, rising, he looked between his legs.

Leisurely he lay down with head toward the sun and put fore paws over his eyes as though starting a game of hide-and-seek and expected the shadow to hide. But this may have been to shut the dazzling sun-glare from his eyes, for presently he moved his head to one side to watch the shadow.

Abruptly he ended, rose to his feet, and started off briskly in the direction he was traveling in when the blue shadow upon the snow coaxed him to stop and play.

Generally the grizzly plays alone. Most animals play with one or many others of their species. Three or four times I have seen a lone grizzly playing much after the manner of a dog—playing with himself as it were. He ran round and round in a small circle, alternating this with leaping into the air and dodging about, and rolling on his back with feet waving in the air. He ended the play with a lively and enthusiastic chase of his tail.

The two cubs that I raised were always eager for play. They played with each other, they were ready at all times to play with me, and occasionally one of them played with my dog Scotch. Grizzlies in captivity will sometimes play with their keeper. Perhaps they would do so more frequently if they liked the keeper. Sometimes pet bears will play with strangers. They are ready to seize an opportunity for brief play and in this, as with the man who was impersonating bears, they often show a sense of humor; and they sometimes imitate or mock the actions of some other animal.

An outing in northwestern Arizona gave me fresh glimpses into grizzly life, although I had not expected to see grizzlies. I found them apparently at home with heat and sand in the edge of a desert. Perhaps these bears were only visitors. They were not dwarfed by the harsh conditions but appeared similar to grizzlies of other localities.

I was sheltered to the leeward of a rock-outcrop waiting for a roaring desert windstorm to subside. As I looked off into the dusty distance, a brown, dust-covered grizzly came into view. He climbed up and sat down upon a large sand-dune and looked around evidently glad that things were clearing. He watched closely a dust spiral which came spinning across the clear sky. As it passed close to him, a withered cactus-lobe dropped from it upon the dune, turned over once or twice, and then rolled down the slope. The grizzly took after it, striking out with right fore paw; but, missing, was upon it with a plunge. Picking the cactus up cautiously in his teeth, he held it for a second, then with a jerk of his head tossed it into the air and pursued it. The sloping sand-dune caved and slid beneath him. Forgetting the cactus, he leaped along the crumbling sand and made a number of lunges, each followed by a dive and an abrupt stop on the sand. He ran in a circle round the crest of the dune several times, occasionally coming to a sudden stop. Then, sliding down the dune, suddenly stopped his play.

He stood still at the foot of the dune for several seconds and looked off into the distance. He was debating what he should do next. Off he started slowly toward the horizon. Into the edge of the mysterious landscape of a mirage he walked and vanished. I thought him lost and rose to move on, when a purple shadowy landscape pushed up into the sky and in this strange, dim scene a giant shadowy grizzly raced and played.

Play is a common habit of animals. Darwin, Wallace, and others have emphasized its importance as a progressive evolutionary factor in the survival of the fittest. Play is rest and relaxation; it gives power and proficiency; it stimulates the brain to the highest pitch of keenness and arouses all the faculties to be eager and at their best; it develops the individual. Play not only is a profound advant-

age to the player, but is necessary to the requirements of an efficient life.

All alert animals freshen themselves with play.
The human race is beginning to do intelligently
what it once did instinctively; it is relearning the
lost art, the triumphant habit, of play.

Matching Wits with the Grizzly

IN April, 1904, "Old Mose," an outlaw grizzly, was killed on Black Mountain, Colorado. For thirty-five years he had kept up his cattle-killing depredations. During this time he was often seen and constantly hunted, and numerous attempts were made to trap him. His home territory was about seventy-five miles in diameter and lay across the Continental Divide. He regularly killed cattle, horses, sheep, and hogs in this territory, and, so far as known, did not leave this region even briefly. Two missing toes on his left hind foot were the means of identifying his track.

Old Mose killed at least five men and eight hundred cattle, together with dozens of colts and other live stock. His damage must have exceeded thirty thousand dollars. Often he smashed the fences that were in his way. He had a fiendish habit of slipping up on campers or prospectors, then rushing into their camp with a roar, and he evidently enjoyed the stampedes thus caused. On these occasions he made no attempt to attack. Although he slaughtered stock to excess, he never went out and attacked people. The five men whom he killed were men who had cornered him and were attempting to kill him.

Rarely do grizzlies kill cattle or big game. Old Mose was an exception. None of the other grizzlies in the surrounding mountains killed live stock. During his last years Old Mose was followed at a distance by a "cinnamon" bear of large size. This grizzly had nothing to do with the killing, never associated with Old Mose, but simply fed on the abundance which he left behind.

A heavy price on his head led the most skillful hunters and trappers to try for Old Mose. Three of the best hunters were killed by him. All trapping schemes failed; so, too, did attempts to poison. Finally he was cornered by a pack of dogs, and the hunter ended his career with the eighth shot.

Though Old Mose was forty or more years of age when killed, his teeth were sound, his fur was in good condition, and he had every appearance of being in excellent health. He was apparently good for several years more of vigorous life.

Trapping the grizzly has become a non-essential occupation. It is a waste of energy, because rarely successful. Now and then a bear is trapped, but it is usually a young bear of but little experience, a mother who is trying to protect her cubs, or a bear whose momentary curiosity caused him to forget his customary caution.

Formerly it was not difficult to trap a grizzly. But he quickly learned to avoid the menace of traps. The bear sees through all the camouflage of the trapper. Deodorized and concealed traps, traps near the bait and far from it, traps placed singly and in clusters—these, and even the slender concealed string of a spring gun, he usually detects and avoids.

I spent a number of days with a trapper who felt certain that he would secure the thousand-dollar reward for the capture of an outlaw cattle-killing grizzly. Earlier than usual the cattlemen drove the cattle from the summer range. The trapper took an old cow to a selected spot near the end of a gulch, picketed her, and surrounded her with spring guns and traps. The outer line of defense consisted of three spring guns which guarded three avenues of approach to the cow. The strings to these guns were of silk line stretched over bushes and tall grass so as to be inconspicuous. As the bear would be likely to seize the cow's head or neck, a trap was set between her head and a large boulder near by. There was a trap on each side of the cow and one behind her.

The first night there was a light fall of snow, but no bear. But the second night he came. Tracks showed that he scented or heard the cow from afar—more than a mile away—and came straight for her. He stopped within two feet of the silk line and walked cautiously round it until he completed the circuit. But there was no opening. He then leaped the line—something I had never before heard of a bear doing. He approached the cow, then walked round her; he went close to the traps and detected just where each one was concealed. Then, between the trap in front and the one on the left, he seized and killed the cow. After feeding on her he dragged the carcass across two traps and left it. Leaping the line again, he went off down stream in the gulch.

The trapper reset the traps the following day and placed an additional one just inside the line, at the point where the grizzly had leaped over it. Then, some distance down stream, he strung a line across the gulch and attached a spring gun to one end of the line.

The grizzly returned that night, coming down the gulch. After walking the lines around the carcass, and apparently having detected the new trap inside, he leaped the line at another point. He avoided the traps and ate about half the remainder of the carcass. Then he piled a few dead logs on what was left, leaped the line again, and went down the gulch. He stopped within ten or twelve feet of the line here and followed it along to where it connected with the rifle on the side of the gulch. Walking round the rifle, he went back into the gulch and followed his trail of the preceding night.

The trapper, amazed, vowed vengeance. He made haste and built a log pen around the remains of the carcass. He then set two traps in the entrance of the pen, one in front of the entrance and one inside the pen.

The second night following, the bear returned, leaped over the line, and cautiously approached the pen. The boulder formed part of the rear end of this. Climbing on top of the boulder, the bear tore off the upper part of the pen, which rested on the boulder, and then, from the boulder, without getting into the pen, reached down and dragged up the carcass. In doing this one of the poles which had been torn out of place and thrown to one side struck the top of a stump, turned over, and fell across the line attached to a spring gun. This fired its waiting shot. Then the grizzly did this astounding thing. He appears to have been on top of the boulder when the shot was fired, but he descended, made his way to the smelly gun, and then examined it, the snow being tracked up in front of it. Returning to the carcass, he dragged it off the boulder and ate the last mouthful. Leaving the bones where they lay, he walked across the line where the pole rested on it and went off up the gulch.

A grizzly is wary for the preservation of his life. It is generally a triumph of stalking to get within short range of him. His senses detect danger afar. He will sometimes hear the stealthy approach of a hunter at the distance of a quarter of a mile, and under favorable conditions he will scent a man at a distance of a mile or more. Being ever on guard, and generally in a place where he can scout with scent, sight, or hearing, he usually manages to keep out of range or under cover. It is not uncommon for two or three hunters in different parts of bear territory, searching with field-glasses, watching from high places, taking advantage of the wind, and moving silently, to spend a week without even seeing a bear, although bears were about. Many times, even when trailed with dogs, through his brains, his endurance, and his ability to move rapidly over rough territory, the grizzly escapes being cornered.

I have often been in bear territory for days without seeing one. Then again I have seen two or more in a few hours. Frequently I have been able to watch a grizzly at moderately short range for an hour or longer. I was chiefly concerned to get near enough to study his actions, and not to take a shot, as I trailed without a gun. But many a day I have failed to see a grizzly, though I searched carefully in a territory which I knew and where the habits of the individual bears were somewhat known to me.

A grizzly territory is covered with a web of dim trails over which he usually travels. If surprised, the grizzly turns and retreats over the trail on which he was advancing. A bear's trail, close behind him, is a dangerous place to be in if he does retreat. Many a hunter, a few feet off the trail, has had the alarmed bear rush by without noticing him, while others, who were directly on the trail, have been run over or assailed by the bear.

When in a trap or cornered, a wounded grizzly

sometimes feigns death. Apparently, when he considers his situation desperate, he sees in this method the possibility of throwing his assailant off his guard. A trapper once invited me to go the rounds with him along his string of traps. In one of these was a young grizzly. At short range the hunter fired two shots and the bear fell in a heap.

We advanced within a few feet and saw that the bear was bleeding freely, but halted "to be sure he was dead." "I make it a point," said the hunter, "to wait until a bear dies before I start skinning him. Once I made the mistake of putting down my rifle and starting to skin the bear before he was dead."

We stepped forward, and the hunter prodded the bear with the end of the rifle-barrel. Like a jumping-jack the bear sprang at the hunter, knocked him over backwards, tore a hole through his clothing, and ripped a bad wound in his skin on the thigh. Fortunately the chain and clog on the trap held the bear from following up his assault.

On another occasion I was with a party of mounted hunters with dogs who chased a grizzly out of his territory and cornered him in a deep box canyon. He was at bay and the excited dogs were harrying him as we came up. He stood in the end of the canyon, facing out, evidently watching for an opportunity to escape. He discouraged all attacks by his swift and cool-headed defense. If a bush stirred behind he made a feint to strike. If a dog came close to his side he appeared to strike without looking. He did not allow any rear movements or attacks to divert his attention from the front, where the hunters stood at short range with rifles ready. They waited for a chance to shoot without hitting a dog. Suddenly the grizzly charged and all was confusion. With a stroke of fore paw he broke the jaw of one horse, with another stroke he caved in three ribs of another horse, he bit and broke a man's arm, disemboweled one dog and wrecked another, and made his safe get-away. Not a shot had been fired. There was no pursuit.

While with three hunters, I once came close upon a grizzly who was digging for mice. The hunters opened fire. For seconds the canyon walls crashed and echoed from the resounding rattling gunnery. Thirty or forty shots were fired. The bear escaped. A hunter took up the trail and the following day ran down the bear and killed him. He carried no wounds except the one from the shot fired by this hunter. He weighed perhaps five hundred pounds.

But the story of the shooting as told by one of the first three hunters was something like this: "We came upon the largest grizzly that I had ever seen. He must have weighed fifteen hundred pounds or more. He was busy digging in an opening and didn't see us until we opened on him at short range. As we had time, we aimed carefully, and each of us got in several shots before he reached the woods. He ran with as much strength as if nothing had happened; yet we simply filled him full of lead—made a regular lead mine of him."

The grizzly is not an exceedingly difficult animal to kill if shot in a vital spot—in the upper part of the heart, in the brain, or through the centre of the shoulder into the spine. Hunters too often fire aimlessly, or become so frightened that they do not even succeed in hitting the bear, though firing shot after shot in his general direction.

William H. Wright once killed five bears with five shots in rapid succession. I was with a hunter in a berry-patch when four grizzlies fell with four lightning-like shots. George McClelland in Wyoming killed nine bears inside of a minute. He probably fired sixteen shots. These were grizzlies, two of which were cubs.

During the last few seconds of his life, after the grizzly receives a fatal wound, he sometimes fights in an amazingly effective and deadly manner. As an old bear-hunter once said, "the grizzly is likely to do a lot of execution after he is nominally dead." Hundreds of hunters have been wounded and scores of others killed by grizzles which they were trying to kill or capture. Hundreds of others have escaped death or serious injury by extremely narrow margins.

A grizzly appears to have caused the death of the first white man to die within the bounds of Colorado. This happened on the plains in the eastern part of the State. Seeing the grizzly in the willows near camp, the man went out to kill him. The wounded grizzly knocked him down and mauled him so severely that he died.

In southern Colorado I saw a frightened hunter on horseback pursued by a mother grizzly. He was chasing her cubs, when she suddenly charged him. The horse wheeled and ran. Although the hunter urged the horse to its utmost, the bear was almost upon them when his dogs rushed in and distracted her.

Hunters claim that if a man feign death when knocked down by a grizzly he is not likely to be injured. James Capen Adams appears to have saved himself a number of times by this method. I have not had occasion to try the experiment.

An old bear-hunter told me that he once saved himself from what seemed to be certain death, in a most unusual manner. A grizzly knocked him sprawling, then leaped upon him to chew him up. In falling, however, the hunter had grabbed up a stone. With this he struck the bear a smashing blow on the tip of his nose as the bear landed upon him. The bear backed off with a roar of pain. This gave the hunter opportunity to seize his rifle and fire a fatal shot.

Three or four men who have been severely bitten and shaken by grizzlies have testified that they felt no pain at the time from these injuries. I cannot account for this. Livingstone, the African explorer, also states that he felt no pain when a lion was chewing him.

I once witnessed a grizzly-roping in Montana that had rare fighting and adventure in it. Two cowboys pursued a grizzly nearly to camp, when several others came riding out with whirling ropes seeking fun. They roped the bear; but a horse was pulled off his feet and dragged, a cowboy was ditched into a bunch of cactus, another cowboy lost his saddle, the cinches giving way under the strain, and a horse struck in the flank had to be shot. Meantime the bear got away and stampeded the entire herd of cattle.

Bear stories have a fascination all their own. Here is one of five men who were hunting in northwestern Montana, a section of high and rugged mountain-peaks, snow-fields, and glaciers, well-nigh inaccessible, and wholly uninhabited save by wild animals. Two of the men went off to a distant glacier-basin for big game, separating and going on opposite sides of a ridge. One of them after a steep climb came upon a grizzly cub, so large as to appear full-grown except to the most careful observer. He killed the bear with three cartridges from his Mauser rifle, and then, leaning the rifle against a rock, stooped over to examine his prize. Suddenly he heard a fearsome cry and a swift rush. Turning, he saw the mother bear coming for him and not more than sixty feet away.

Springing to his rifle, he put two steel-clad bullets into the grizzly, emptying his gun. With remarkable coolness he slipped in another cartridge and sent a third bullet into her. But Mauser bullets are small and an enraged grizzly is a hard thing to stop. The three bullets did not stop this mother bear, frantic at the sight of her dead cub. With one stroke of her paw she knocked the hunter into a gulch, eight feet below. Then she sprang down after him, caught him in her mouth, shook him as a dog might shake a doll, and dropped him. She caught him up again, his face between her tusks, shook him, and again dropped him. A third time she snatched him up. But now the little Mauser bullets had done their work, and she fell dead across the hunter's feet.

It was high time, for the man was in little better condition than the bear. His scalp and cheek and throat were torn open, there were five gaping wounds in his chest, his thigh bore an irregular tear two or three inches wide from which the flesh hung in ragged strips, and his left wrist was broken and the bones protruding through the twisted flesh. His companion, alarmed by the six shots, hurried to the hunter. He bound up his wounds, set him on a horse, guided him for two hours across country without a trail, and got him to camp at nightfall. But to save the man's life it was necessary to get him to the railroad in short order. He was put on a horse with a man on each side to support him, and for eleven hours the party climbed down the five miles through forest and jungle, cutting their way as they went. At dark, completely exhausted, they flagged a limited train. The hunter was hurried to a hospital and operated upon and his life saved.

The man with a gun is a specialist. He is looking for a particular thing in order to kill it. Generally the gun hampers full enjoyment of the wilderness. The hunter misses most of the beauty and the glory of the trail. If he stops to enjoy the pranks of other animals, or to notice the color of cloud or flower, he will miss his opportunity to secure his game. When at last he is within range of a bear, it may scent him and be off at any minute, so he must shoot at once. He learns but little of the character of the animal.

Trailing the grizzly without a gun is the very acme of hunting. The gunless hunter comes up close, but he lingers to watch the bear and perhaps her cubs. He sees them play. Often, too, he has the experience of seeing wilderness etiquette when other bears or animals come into the scene. The information that he gathers and his enjoyment excel those obtained by the man with a gun.

Roosevelt has said and shown that the hunter whose chief interest is in shooting has but little out of the hunt. Audubon did a little shooting for specimens. Wright had as many thrills with the camera as with the rifle. Adams was far happier and more useful with his live grizzlies than he was killing other grizzlies. Emerson McMillin was satisfied to hunt without either gun or camera. The words and sketches of Ernest Thompson Seton have given us much of the artistic side of the wilderness. Dr. Frank M. Chapman explored two continents for the facts of bird-lore and in addition to his books prepared the magnificent bird-groups in the American Museum of Natural History. Thoreau enjoyed life in the wilderness without a gun. But John Muir was the supreme wilderness hunter and wanderer. He never carried a gun. Usually he was in the wilds alone. He spent years in a grizzly bear country. But the wealth of nature-lore with which he enriched his books make him the Shakespeare of nature.

The man without a gun can enjoy every scene of nature along his way. He has time to turn aside for other animals, or to stop and watch any one of the countless unexpected wild-life exhibitions that are ever appearing. Then, too, he hears the many calls and sounds, the music of the wilds. The wild places, especially in grizzly bear land, are crowded with plants and with exhibitions of the manners and the customs of animals, and are rich in real nature stories being lived with all their charm and their dramatic changes.

Where Curiosity Wins

THE grizzly bear has the most curiosity of any animal that I have watched. As curiosity arises from the desire to know, it appears that the superior mentality of the grizzly may be largely due to the alertness which curiosity sustains.

Although the grizzly has learned the extreme danger of exposing himself near man, yet, at times, all his vigilant senses are temporarily hypnotized by curiosity. On rare occasions it betrays him into trouble, or lands a cub in a trap. In old bears curiosity is accompanied with a keenness of observation and a caution that enable him to satisfy his desire for information without exposure to danger. Often it enables him to anticipate a concealed danger—to penetrate the camouflage of something dangerous. Curiosity prevents oncoming events from being thrust on the curious. It is an effort to obtain advance information instead of taking things as they come.

In 1826 Drummond, the botanist, collected plants in the Rocky Mountains. In stopping to examine, to gather, and to press them he was doing the unusual. He thus attracted the attention of numerous grizzlies, who even came close to watch him. They showed no inclination to attack. Bears are "chock-full of curiosity" and will sometimes forget to eat in trying to understand at once the new or the unusual.

Lewis and Clark tell of a bear on a sand-bar who showed interest in their boat as it passed. He raised himself on hind feet and looked after them, and then plunged into the river and swam toward the boat. This novel outfit should have attracted the attention of any living thing, and a curious grizzly must have been almost overcome with wonder. Yet the explorers erroneously assumed that this intense curiosity and consequent attempt for closer inspection was evidence of ferocity. During the first fifty years of the white man's contact with the grizzly, the bear frequently came close to a man or a camp for a better look; most frontiersmen thought this near approach was ferocity in the bear. Often the bear was greeted with bullets, and in due time he learned to satisfy his curiosity by stealth instead of by direct approach. But inquisitive he still is.

In crossing the mountains in northern New Mexico I was overtaken by a Swede on his way to a lumber-camp. He carried a pack, and a part of it was an accordion. We made camp that night near the head of a gulch. Across from us a treeless mountain rose a thousand feet.

After supper the Swede played on his accordion and was soon lost in music. Pausing in my note-making to enjoy his contented expression, I saw an old grizzly watching us from across the mountain. Standing upon a boulder, he was looking over the tops of the spruce trees that thrust up out of the gulch. Through my field-glasses he appeared even more lost in wonder at the music than the enthusiastic, emotional player. When the refrain died away, the grizzly climbed down off the boulder, and then, as another piece was begun, at once rose to remount, but instead stood with fore paws against the boulder, listening. By and by he started up the mountain, pausing every few steps to turn and listen. He either stood broadside, his head tilted sideways, or raised himself on tiptoe, fascinated. A loud, lively, clashing close to one piece started him off on a gallop, but as soon as the music stopped the bear paused. He appeared puzzled and fidgeted about while the player sat silent, listening to my description of the bear's movements. A soft and melodious piece was next played. The bear, as the first strain sounded on the evening air, seated himself on his haunches facing us, and thus remained until the piece was finished. Then he climbed higher up the mountain and, on reaching the sky-line, walked lingering along in the last rays of the sun, looking down on us now and then as though wanting more music.

For two or three hours I watched a number of water-ouzels in the St. Vrain River. They often came within three or four feet of where I sat on the bank with my back against a large boulder. To avoid frightening them, I sat motionless, not turning even my head for an hour or more at a time. I was enjoying their actions, when suddenly I caught the distinct odor of a bear. While still motionless and wondering further about this new interest, I heard the faint crack of a stick behind me. Turning my head at this sound, I saw a grizzly raised on hind legs with fore paws resting on top of the boulder against which I was leaning. He looked at me with intense interest, all caution forgotten. His curiosity absolutely dominated. But my slight movement had aroused him. In two seconds from the time I turned he was crashing off through the thicket and probably was condemning himself for being so curious.

One Sunday afternoon one of the men in a lumber-camp rigged up a canvas hammock from the remnants of an old tent and suspended it between two trees. A pet grizzly who belonged at the camp watched him with curious interest while he worked. She observed him with still greater interest as he stretched himself out in it and began reading. When the man deserted the hammock, she walked up to it, struck it, pushed it back and forth with fore paws, and then began rather awkwardly to climb into it. She had almost succeeded, when her weight upon the edge caused it to tip over and spill her on the ground. She leaped back surprised, then walked round the hammock, eyeing it with great curiosity. But the second attempt at climbing into the hammock was successful, and she made a most comical and awkward sight stretched out in it flat upon her back.

I came upon a grizzly on the heights above the timber-line watching the progress of a forest fire. Squatted on his haunches like a dog, he was intently watching the fire-front below. A deep roar at one place, high leaping flames at another, a vast smoke-cloud at another caused him to turn toward each with rapt attention. He followed with eager eyes, also, the swiftly advancing cloud-shadows as they mysteriously rushed forward over ridge and valley. So intent was he that none of his keen senses warned him of my presence, though I stood near for two or three minutes, watching him. When I called he slowly turned his head. He stared at me in a half-dazed manner, then angrily showed his teeth. After another second he fled like a frightened rabbit.

The actions of a fisherman were being followed with the closest attention by a grizzly when I came along the opposite side of a narrow canyon. The bear stood still for some minutes, all his faculties concentrated on the fisherman. Every cast of the fly was observed with the greatest interest. A dangling trout caused him much excitement. Possibly the wind, touched with man-scent, finally warned him of danger. Anyway, he suddenly came to his senses, roused himself, and ran off.

On one of my camping-trips into the mountains I carried a long yellow slicker. Wearing this one misty, half-snowy day, I was followed by a grizzly. Twice he evidently came close to me; although I did not see him, I scented him. When well upon a mountain during the afternoon, I crossed an open place in the woods where a breeze broke up the low-drifting clouds. For a moment I beheld a much interested grizzly near by. He stood and stared at me with all caution forgotten in his curiosity about the long yellow coat.

At dark I made camp at timber-line and forgot about the bear. The slicker was hung over a pole against a cliff to drain and dry. I went to sleep about eleven o'clock, after writing up my notes and watching my camp-fire. During the night the grizzly came boldly into camp, reared up, and slit the slicker. My shoes near by had not been noticed; the bacon and raisins swinging from a limb had not interested his keen nose. He was interested only in that slicker.

This was a case where the grizzly's curiosity might have got him into trouble. So intent was he on seeing this one thing that for hours he had forgotten food-hunting and followed me; and then in order to have a closer examination of it he must have waited near my camp two or three hours until I had lain down.

Another time, in the Yellowstone, while I was sleeping out, a big grizzly who had followed me all day came to give me closer inspection. I was awakened by his lightly clawing my bed. I opened my eyes and watched him for some seconds and lay perfectly still while he sniffed me over. After several seconds of this he appeared to have satisfied his curiosity and walked quietly away beneath the stars.

As I was trying to flash information with a looking-glass from Mount Lincoln to a prospector down in the valley one day, a grizzly became attracted by the flashes and lay down to watch them circle and shimmer here and there. In the San Juan Mountains a prospector once lost a wheel from a rude cart which he was hauling up a steep, roadless slope. As the detached wheel went bounding down and across the bottom of the gulch, a grizzly hit an attitude of attention and watched it. He became excited as it leaped and rushed up the opposite slope, and when it rolled over he approached cautiously to see what manner of thing it might be. A grizzly sat down on his haunches to watch the uncertain movements of an umbrella which had taken advantage of a wind-storm to desert a mountain-top artist. He observed the disheveled umbrella with the greatest enjoyment as it danced across the moorland, and was particularly interested when a whirl sent it high into the air.

Riding a lazy pony slowly, silently, along a trail in the San Juan Mountains, I came close upon a grizzly and three cubs. They aroused the deep emotional nature of my pony. He took on new and fiery life, and in his eagerness to reach a high mountain across the canyon he forgot all about the topography—the canyon that lay deep between. While he was standing on one hind foot on the edge of the canyon I leaped from the saddle. The old bear and cubs, forgetting all possible danger, while he was thus performing stood up to watch the entire exhibition.

A grizzly keeps an eye on near-by animals, often without appearing to do so. But if the animal is doing something new or unusual he gives it his entire attention. Two bears, side by side, are interested in the same thing; yet the individuality of each will show if you watch them a minute. Of course, all bears are not equally curious about the same thing, but seldom do I recall outwitting a bear even when appealing to his curiosity, and never could I class him as stupid.

Grizzlies in regions just invaded by white men appear to have put in much time trying to make out what these strange creatures were about. What man is doing is ever of first importance to the long-lived grizzly. His interest in his surroundings appears to be greater than that of the average person. At any rate, the grizzly shows better knowledge of the habits of human beings than people have of the habits of bears.

His is not the curiosity of the idle; the grizzly is not prying into the affairs of others for mere pastime, but is concerned only so far as these affairs may benefit or harm him. His is the intelligent curiosity of a mind seeking facts. Most of the time he leads a solitary life; he rarely exchanges ideas or information with other bears. Most animals live in pairs or flocks and, each gathering information for all, they divide sentinel duty; but single-handed the grizzly must get the news, must scout for himself. He is ever on the watch, does nothing blindly, and he simply must understand.

Any unusual occurrence arouses a grizzly's curiosity, and is to him "a word to the wise." His success lies in constant alertness. He might well be

likened to a frontiersman; he has that painstaking
vigilance, that untiring energy, which seeks to discover whether this strange track, sound, or displace-
ment is the camouflage which conceals the enemy or if it be a clue which will lead to something
of advantage. He at once endeavors to find out all
that may be learned about it.

The grizzly bear may have inherited a love for
exploration. His ancestors were adventurers, coming
to this continent from Asia. The natural attraction
which the new and unusual has for him may generally be gratified in his curiosity about things at
home. But we may readily imagine that the grizzly
must sometimes become restless when there is
nothing stirring near by, when he finds no excitement in his home territory, and so wanders like an
explorer to seek discoveries in far-off scenes. He is
innately an adventurer; he seeks adventure and often finds it. His curiosity does not allow him to live
in a rut—to live contentedly with old conditions.
He is always learning; he keeps alive and growing.

The grizzly bear simply cannot be understood,
nor half understood, if his curiosity is not considered. Notice a grizzly bear pet, observe a grizzly in
a zoo, watch both the cubs and the old grizzlies in
the Yellowstone and Glacier National Parks. They
walk about like superior animals, which they are.
Those in parks ever notice any sudden movement,
any new figure in the foreground, and detect any
unusual noise that comes from far away behind the
woods. The grizzly bear and the scout are masters
of woodcraft through intensive observation. Behind
the word curiosity the grizzly bear has put a world
of meaning.

The wild grizzly shows a deeper feeling for the
scenes, the sounds, and the movements around him

than any other animal that I have watched. Sometimes, while thus interested, he sits on haunches like a dog, again he stands on all fours, at other times he stands on hind feet, tiptoe, and, on rare occasions, he sits on his tail with fore paws against his breast, perhaps leaning against something. Once in a while he gives full attention while lying down.

When looking at scenery and sunsets, his appearance is one of enjoyment; he appears to have feeling in the conscious presence of that which we call beautiful or glorious. I have seen a grizzly looking at a magnificent and many-colored sunset, completely absorbed. There was no fear at a flash of lightning or the roar and echoing roll of thunder. Once I saw a grizzly turn to stare at the course of a shooting star; another gazed for seconds at a brilliant rainbow.

Generally the grizzly's attention to these demonstrations rose superior to commonplace curiosity; he looked long, he listened closely, he was absorbed, and he appeared to feel as he sat lost in wonder. Had he been a child, with the power of speech, he certainly would have asked questions. Often his expression, his attitude, indicated that he was saying to himself: "What was that? What caused it? Where did that noise come from? What are those strange shadows running from, and how can they move without a sound?"

On the Defensive

IN the grizzly bear we have the leading animal of North America, and one who might well be put at the head of the wild life of the earth. He has brain and brawn. He is self-contained and is prepared for anything. He makes an impressive appearance. He looks capable. He has bulk, agility, strength, endurance, repose, courage, enthusiasm, and curiosity. He is a masterful fighter if forced to defend himself.

But, a century ago, fifty years ago, or to-day, one could ramble the grizzly's territory in safety—unless attempting to kill a grizzly. The grizzly objects to being killed. If he is surprised or crowded so that he sees no escape, if the cubs are in danger or the mother thinks they are, or if the bear is wounded, there will be a fight or a retreat; and the grizzly will not be the one retreating. Almost every animal—wild or domestic—will fight if cornered or if he thinks himself cornered.

Before the days of the repeating rifle the grizzly boldly wandered over his domain as absolute master; there was nothing for him to fear; not an aggressive foe existed. But, being ever curious, he hastened to examine whatever interested him. The novel outfit of Lewis and Clark, which appears to have attracted unusual attention even from frontier people, must naturally have aroused the highest pitch of interest in the numbers of bears congregated in places along the river. There were boats of odd type—some with sails—strange cargoes, men in picturesque accoutrements, and even a colored man. The frequent close approaches which the bears made in trying to satisfy their curiosity caused Lewis and Clark to think them ferocious.

But is the grizzly bear ferocious? All the first-hand evidence I can find says he is not. Speaking from years of experience with him my answer is emphatically, "No!" Nearly every one whom a grizzly has killed went out with the special intention of killing a grizzly. The majority of people who hold the opinion that he is not ferocious are those who have studied him without attempting to kill him; while the majority who say that he is ferocious are those who have killed or attempted to kill him.

During the greater part of my life I have lived in a grizzly bear region. I have camped for months alone and without a gun in their territory. I have seen them when alone and when with hunters, in Colorado, Utah, Arizona, Mexico, Wyoming, Montana, Idaho, Washington, British Columbia, and Alaska. I have spent weeks trailing and watching grizzlies, and their tracks in the snow showed that they often trailed me. They frequently came close, and there were times when they might have attacked me with every advantage. But they did not do so. As they never made any attack on me, nor on any one else that I know of who was not bent on killing them, I can only conclude that they are not ferocious.

Once I was running down a Wyoming mountainside, leaping fallen fire-killed timber, when suddenly I surprised a grizzly by landing within a few feet of him. He leaped up and struck at me with sufficient force to have almost cut me in two had the blow landed. Then he instantly fled. This, however, was not ferocity. Plainly he thought himself attacked and struck in self-defense.

There are many naturalists and frontiersmen who affirm from first-hand experience that the grizzly is not ferocious, and following are given a number of quotations from a few of these men.

John Muir, who spent about forty years in the wilderness home of the grizzly bear, from 1868 to 1912, usually camped alone and never carried firearms. He has repeatedly called attention in his books to the wilderness as a place of safety, and has mentioned that grizzly bears are masters in attending to their own affairs; also that bears have effectively suggested to wilderness visitors to do likewise. In "Our National Parks" Muir says:

"In my first interview with a Sierra bear we were frightened and embarrassed, both of us, but the bear's behavior was better than mine. ... After studying his appearance as he stood at rest, I rushed forward to frighten him, that I might study his gait in running. But, contrary to all I had heard about the shyness of bears, he did not run at all; and when I stopped short within a few steps of him, as he held his ground in a fighting attitude, my mistake was monstrously plain. I was put on my good behavior, and never afterwards forgot the right manners of the wilderness."

Muir also says, in "Steep Trails":

"There are bears in the woods, but not in such numbers nor of such unspeakable ferocity as town-dwellers imagine, nor do bears spend their lives in going about the country like the devil, seeking whom they may devour. Oregon bears, like most others, have no liking for man either as meat or as society; and while some may be curious at times to see what manner of creature he is, most of them have learned to shun people as deadly enemies."

Mr. William H. Wright spent most of his time from 1883 to 1908 as a hunter of wild animals, and especially as a hunter of the grizzly. In addition to being an observer of exceptional care while hunting and trapping, he spent some years in photographing grizzlies. He first studied them in order to hunt them successfully; then laid aside his rifle and hunted them to study them. From full acquaintance with the grizzly Mr. Wright declares that he is not ferocious. He offers the following comment concerning his curiosity—a trait which early explorers mistook for ferocity:

"We know now that the grizzly is chock-full of curiosity, and that one of his habits is to follow up any trail that puzzles or interests him, be it of man or beast. This trait has been noted and misconstrued by many. ... So often have I seen this curiosity and proved it to be innocent that I have no fear whatever of these animals when indulging in this weakness of theirs. Time and again I have allowed one to approach within a few yards of me, and no calm observer who had watched a bear defying his own caution to satisfy his own inquisitiveness could mistake the nature of his approach."

Drummond, the botanist, had numerous experiences with grizzlies in the Rocky Mountains in 1826. He was familiar with their curiosity. He says that often they came close and stood up to look at him. But if he made a noise with his specimen-box, or "even waved his hand," they ran away.

James Capen Adams hunted and trapped big game from 1849 to 1859 in California and along the Pacific Coast. He captured numerous grizzlies, both old and young, and literally domesticated them. He discusses their characteristics at length. He knew them intimately, and in summing them up after years of close association he says of the grizzly, "He did not invite combat."

Kit Carson, another frontiersman of long experience with grizzlies, in writing of them does not call them ferocious.

Dr. W. T. Hornaday knows the grizzly in the wilds and has long and intimately known him in the zoo. In "The American Natural History" Dr. Hornaday has the following:

"I have made many observations on the temper of the Grizzly Bear, and am convinced that naturally the disposition of this reputedly savage creature is rather peaceful and good-natured. At the same time, however, no animal is more prompt to resent an affront or injury, or punish an offender. The Grizzly temper is defensive, not aggressive; and unless the animal is cornered, or *thinks he is cornered*, he always flees from man."

The early explorers were warned by the Indians that the grizzly was "an awful and ferocious animal." All the early writers had the preconceived belief that the grizzly was ferocious. Many of these writers never saw a grizzly, but wrote down as fact the erroneous conclusions of the Indians. The few writers who did see a grizzly evidently judged him largely from these preconceived ideas. Even Lewis and Clark describe a number of the grizzly's actions and call him ferocious when the very actions which they describe simply show him as being curious, interested, or, at worst, excited at their strange appearance. They misinterpreted what actually happened.

A few sentences from Audubon well illustrate the wrought-up frame of mind of many hunters and authors when hunting or writing about the grizzly. Audubon says:

"While in the neighborhood where the grizzly bear may possibly be hidden, the excited nerves will cause the heart's pulsations to quicken if but a startled ground squirrel run past, the sharp click of the lock is heard and the rifle hastily thrown to the shoulder before a second of time has assured the hunter of the trifling cause of his emotion." This suggests emotion but not accuracy.

In summing up the animals of the North and West in 1790, Edward Umfreville wrote of the "red and the grizzle bear" that "their nature is savage and ferocious, their power dangerous, and their haunts to be guarded against."

In 1795 Sir Alexander MacKenzie recorded the following:

"The Indians entertain great apprehension of this kind of a bear, which is called the grisly bear, and they never venture to attack it except in a party of least three or four."

Henry M. Brackenridge, author of "Views of Louisiana," wrote the following from hearsay:

"This animal is the monarch of the country which he inhabitates. The African lion or the Bengal tiger are not more terrible than he. He is the enemy of man and literally thirsts for human blood. So far from shunning, he seldom fails to attack and even to hunt him. The Indians make war upon these ferocious monsters with ceremonies as they do upon a tribe of their own species, and, in the recital of their victories, the death of one of them gives the warrior greater renown than the scalp of an enemy. He possesses an amazing strength, and attacks without hesitation and tears to pieces the largest buffalo."

The first paragraph which Lewis and Clark wrote concerning the grizzly, April 29, 1805, says:

"We proceeded early, with a moderate wind. Captain Lewis, who was on shore with one hunter, met about eight o'clock two white bears. Of the strength and ferocity of this animal the Indians had given us dreadful accounts; they never attack him but in parties of six or eight persons, and even then are often defeated with a loss of one or more of the party. Having no weapons but bows and arrows, and the bad guns which the traders supply them, they are obliged to approach very near the bear, and as no wound except through the head or heart is fatal they frequently fall a sacrifice if they miss their aim. He rather attacks than avoids man, and such is the terror which he has inspired that the Indians who go in quest of him paint themselves and perform all the superstitious rites customary when they make war on a neighboring nation. Hitherto those we had seen did not appear desirous of encountering us, but although to a skillful rifleman the danger is very much diminished, yet the white bear is still a terrible animal. On the approach of these two, both Captain Lewis and the hunter fired and each wounded a bear; one of them made his escape; the other turned upon Captain Lewis and pursued him seventy or eighty yards, but being badly wounded he could not run so fast as to prevent him reloading his piece, which he again aimed at him, and a third shot from the hunter brought him to the ground."

Below are two additional paragraphs from the Journal of Lewis and Clark. These show that the grizzly was most wide-awake and curious, and also that he was not accustomed to being afraid.

"The bear which gave so much trouble on the head of the Missouri are equally fierce in this quar-. This morning one of them, which was on a sand-bar as the boat passed, raised himself on his hind feet and after looking at the party, plunged in and swam towards them. He was received with three balls in the body; he then turned around and made for the shore. Towards evening another entered the water to swim across. Captain Clark ordered the boat towards the shore, and just as the bear landed shot the animal in the head. It proved to be the largest female they had ever seen, and so old that its tusks were worn quite smooth."

"Just as he arrived near Willow Run, he approached a thicket of brush in which was a white bear, which he did not discover till he was within ten feet of him; his horse started, and wheeling suddenly round, threw M'Neal almost immediately under the bear, who started up instantly, and finding the bear raising himself on his hind feet to attack him, struck him on the head with the butt end of his musket; the blow was so violent that it broke the breech of the musket and knocked the bear to the ground, and before he recovered, M'Neal, seeing a willow tree close by, sprang up, and there remained while the bear closely guarded the foot of the tree until late in the afternoon. He then went off, and M'Neal being released came down, and having found his horse, which had strayed off to the distance of two miles, returned to camp. These animals are, indeed, of a most extraordinary ferocity, and it is matter of wonder that in all our encounters we have had the good fortune to escape."

The grizzly was introduced to the world by Governor DeWitt Clinton of New York, who appears to have taken his information from the Journal of Lewis and Clark. In the course of an address before the Literary and Philosophical Society of New York City in 1814, he completely misinterpreted the real character of the grizzly and popularized a number of errors that not only were believed then but have survived to this day. The real grizzly is a distinguished character; but the grizzly as commonly described by tongue and story—well, "there ain't no such animal."

Governor Clinton in discussing the work in store for the coming naturalists said, "There is the white, brown, or grizzly bear, the ferocious tyrant of the American woods—it exists, the terror of the savages, the tyrant of all other animals, devouring alike man and beast and defying the attacks of a whole tribe of Indians." Few people realize to what extent these inaccurate words have discouraged outdoor life and how enormously they have contributed to the output of fictitious nature writing.

The Indians had a profound respect for the fighting efficiency of the grizzly. When one of them killed a grizzly he triumphantly wore the claw as a medal for rare bravery. The grizzly has a head and a hide that the Indian could rarely penetrate with either an arrow or a spear. We may readily believe that the grizzly defied the attacks of "a whole tribe of Indians," as Governor DeWitt Clinton said. He would defy a whole tribe of Indians or a score of white men with similar weapons to-day. So, too, would the elephant, the African lion, or the tiger.

With the rifles used at the time of Lewis and Clark it was necessary for the hunter to approach close to the bear that the bullet might have sufficient velocity to penetrate a vital spot. The rifles being only single-shot, the hunter was exposed to the assault of the bear in case his aim missed or the shot was ineffective. It is not surprising that in t cases those attempting to kill the grizzly either were overpowered by him or succeeded only through force of numbers and with the loss of some of the assailants. But the ability of the grizzly to withstand such attacks and to defend himself has been confused with ferocity.

The grizzly is a fighting-machine of the first order and with the weapons of two or three generations ago he often sold his life most dearly. In a short time the grizzly had the reputation of being a terrible fighter, and along with this he was given the reputation of being ferocious—of being an awful hunter of man. For the grizzly to repel effectually those who went out to attack him is a very different thing from his going out to hunt and to attack people who were not molesting him. This latter he has never done.

The words of Umfreville, MacKenzie, Brackenridge, Clinton, and Lewis and Clark bring out strongly that the grizzly is a fighter, formidable, perhaps unequaled. Their opinion on this point is supported by ample first-hand testimony down through the years, from all over the grizzly territory. But it has not been established that the grizzly is ferocious, is seeking to kill. No, the grizzly does not look for a fight; he is for peace at almost any price.

The grizzly fights in self-defense; men do the same. A man is not criminal for fighting in self-defense; neither is a grizzly. For this self-defense fighting the grizzly should not be put in the criminal class. "The worm will turn," is an old saying. All animals fight in self-defense, some more quickly than others. Few ever succeed against man; the grizzly often does. Apparently the effective self-defense of the grizzly is responsible for his criminal reputation.

It is common for those who believe that the grizzly is ferocious to believe also that he eats human flesh. There is no known instance of his having done so.

We are now hearing that the Alaska bears are especially ferocious. Yet, in Alaska at the present time, and for many years in the past, the bear trails are concealed as much as possible by being in the woods. This would prevent the bear on the trail being readily seen by man. Along the sea, where much bear food is cast ashore, the trails are not upon the open beach but some distance away behind the trees. The bears depend on scent to tell them if there is anything along the shore to eat. Both their trails and their daily life in Alaska conclusively show that their chief concern is to keep away from and out of sight of man.

The experience with bears in the Yellowstone Park demonstrates that the grizzly is not ferocious. The Park had a numerous grizzly population when it was made a wild-life reservation. The people who in increasing numbers visited the Park carried no fire-arms and they were not molested by the grizzlies. Yet grizzlies were all about. After some twenty years of this friendly association of people and grizzlies, a number of grizzlies, dyspeptic and demoralized from eating garbage, and annoyed by the teasing of thoughtless people, became cross and lately even dangerous. But these bears cannot be called ferocious. Eliminate the garbage-piles and cease harassing the bears, and they will again be friendly.

The grizzly bear has been a golden gift of the gods for the countless writers of highly colored alleged natural history. There is a type, too, of wild fiction-writers of the Captain Mayne Reid class whose thrilling stories of the grizzly and other wilderness animals are purely fictitious, and, though not even pretending to be fact, appear to have been taken seriously by thousands. So prolific and continuous has been the output of these writers that facts have been lost, and it is practically impossible for the average individual to know the real grizzly bear. This comes near to being the immortality of error. It is a national misfortune that the overwhelming majority of people should be imposed upon with erroneous natural history. The destiny of the human race is intimately tied up with nature, and for any one to misunderstand the simple facts which unite us with nature is to be out of harmony with the whole scheme of things. An accurate knowledge of natural history has an important place in guiding the judgments of our race.

Because of their intimate knowledge of the grizzly bear, James Capen Adams, William H. Wright, and Philip Ashton Rollins admired this animal. It would be a glorious thing if every one appreciated the real character of the grizzly bear. A changed attitude toward him—the great animal of the outdoors—might cause the wilderness to appeal to all as a friendly wonderland.

Man's Loyal Companion

JUST as I reached the edge of the woods by a saw-mill in the Medicine Bow Mountains, a young grizzly rushed at me as though to "chew me up." She frightened me for a second, but the next instant I realized that it was only a bluff.

"You are not polite to strangers," I said to her.

She stood still for a minute, looked at me quietly, and then began leaping and racing about me like an awkward puppy who has just made your acquaintance and is eager for play.

"Miss Grizzly" had been captured when a small cub, about a year and a half before, and raised by the foreman of the mill. The pet and favorite of all the men in camp, she had the freedom of the place, played with the visiting teamsters, and welcomed strangers. She was companionable with every one, but was nobody's grizzly.

Early in her life at the mill she had learned to be afraid of the big buzzing saw. One day as she stood several feet away, either listening to the hum of the saw or watching the dust thrown from it, the saw chanced to strike a knot. A piece of this flew and struck Miss Grizzly solidly between the eyes, raising a lump. She was exceedingly wary of the saw after that. Although she ranged around it, she never risked going too close again. Often she leaped upon a log as it was starting on the carrier for the saw, but she never failed to leap off before getting as near the saw as she had been when struck by the flying chip.

A logger from several miles away who had come

to remain at the mill for some time brought with him his pet black bear. All the men were assembled in the bunk-house to see the meeting of the two bears. Miss Grizzly was in the room when the black bear came in. The instant the black bear caught sight of Miss Grizzly he was "scared out of his wits." He at once turned about and tried to run from the room. But haughty Miss Grizzly acted indifferently. Although she was much smaller than the black, there was no fear; she pretended that she had not seen him. Ignoring him, she went out of the room by the rear door and began playing with one of the dogs.

Miss Grizzly was ever independent, resourceful, and capable. One day a teamster handed her a bottle of catsup. Standing erect, she took it deftly in her fore paws. She was greatly interested in it—probably in the color. In turning it about she caught sight of a floating air-bubble. Inverting the bottle from end to end, she tried to make this out; she held it between her eyes and the light, she shook it back and forth close to her ear. Then, going directly to a near-by log, she brought the bottle down upon it and catsup splashed in all directions. Her curiosity satisfied, she seemed to enjoy licking up the catsup.

The men never teased Miss Grizzly nor attempted to teach her any tricks. Consequently her disposition was uniformly of the best. She enjoyed cartwheeling and liked to have the men start her with a little push down the slope near the mill. Curling her nose behind her toes, she rolled over and over. Occasionally she climbed upon the flat-roofed lumber-shed for the fun of rolling off. While she did much climbing over the logs and lumberpiles and on the low roofs, she did not attempt to climb a tree after the first few weeks she was at the mill.

She was never chained and she rambled about wherever she liked. She spent most of her time at the sawmill or close to it. Occasionally she followed one of the loggers off into the woods. Sometimes by the hour she would lie near where he was working, interested in the flying chips. Sometimes she would go off on a little hunting-excursion, tear an old stump to pieces, or overturn rocks in search of ants and grubs. One day a tree in falling sent a shower of limbs all about Miss Grizzly, one of them apparently striking her. She was not injured, but, bawling like a frightened baby, she turned and ran for camp, and never again did she go to the woods with the logger.

Miss Grizzly was usually fed just outside the cook-house door. She preferred to eat in seclusion. But when especially hungry she came boldly into the dining-room while the men were eating. Walking round the table, she accepted whatever was offered her—and every one offered her something.

She was fond of the teamster who arrived twice a week with supplies and usually followed him homeward, running along behind the wagon. Now and then she preferred to ride close to him with her nose on his shoulder, sitting on her haunches like a big dog. Usually she went only two or three miles and then returned promptly home, but occasionally she lingered. One day, during her third summer at the mill, she followed the teamster as usual but did not return until in the night. After this she made an occasional excursion into the woods alone, sometimes being gone a day or two. One day, after an unusually long absence, she came back accompanied by another young grizzly.

Tracks in the dust showed that the stranger had hesitated to approach the mill. Within two or three hundred yards of it he had reared up, alert, as though he had scented or heard something alarming. Here and there in the road Miss Grizzly had evidently turned back to reassure him. Both finally came within a short distance of the mill, when at the appearance of one of the men the strange bear turned and fled.

The first winter Miss Grizzly did not offer to hibernate. She was fed regularly, and the men never thought of encouraging her to den up. But the second winter she slept three months. About the first of December she dug a den back into the side of the big sawdust pile and crawled in. Two or three times during the winter the men wakened her, and she came to the mouth of the den and then returned to sleep. Once she came out for a few hours, but, though tempted, refused to eat. Ordinarily Miss Grizzley slept outside the sawmill, against one end of the building; but sometimes she spent the night beneath the edge of the slab-pile.

The third autumn at the mill Miss Grizzly made numerous excursions into the woods alone, and one day she went off on one from which she did not return.

BEN FRANKLIN

James Capen Adams, known as "Grizzly Adams," the celebrated hunter and trapper of wild American animals, was easily foremost for what he accomplished in showing the real character of the grizzly bear. His biography, "The Adventures of James Capen Adams," tells of his intelligent, sympathetic, and successful methods in handling grizzly bears, whether they were young or old. He made loyal companions of grizzlies and trained them so that they served him capably in a number of capacities. In the handling of these animals Adams studied their character. He was uniformly sympathetic, kind, calm, and firm. He endeavored to accomplish any desired end through gentleness and by appeal to the animal's interest and loyalty. Force and torture, which so often are the chief equipment of animal-trainers, had no place in his methods.

The story of Ben Franklin and his bringing-up by Adams gives an excellent view of a real grizzly and an excellent master. Adams took Ben Franklin from a den when he was a tiny blind cub. At first he was fed on a mixture of water, flour, and sugar, and then Adams persuaded a greyhound which was nursing a puppy, Rambler, to suckle Ben. Ben, while nursing, was made to wear buckskin mittens to prevent his scratching his foster-mother. Ben and Rambler became lifelong companions, and when not asleep spent most of their time playing and tussling with each other.

Sometimes, when traveling through the mountains with them when they were still small, Adams would take them out of the wagon and allow them to play together. They chased each other over the grass or had merry races after rabbits, squirrels, or prairie-dogs. When older, they enjoyed traveling all day together on foot. On a number of occasions it was necessary for Ben to wear buckskin moccasins to protect his feet from the sharp rocks and the desert sand, and once, after he was much larger, his feet became so sore he was loaded into the wagon and hauled for a day or two.

Ben quickly outstripped his foster-brother in

size, but, although very swift of foot, he was soon outrun by the greyhound. Several times Ben and Rambler came upon the fleet-footed antelope, which Rambler closely pursued for miles. Ben would usually race for half a mile or so, then, being unable to keep up with Rambler, would sit down, look around for a minute, and return to his master. For several years they followed Adams in his long hunting-trips across the mountains.

Adams sometimes tempted Ben by placing within his reach scraps of dainty food, but he was so well trained that he never touched any food until it was given to him. Often, when hungry, Ben would sit on his haunches near his master, occasionally looking up into his face and remonstrating if he did not receive attention.

When Ben became larger, Adams trained him as a pack-animal, and Ben carried the camp outfit and supplies on his back through the wilderness. At other times he was used with Rambler in hunting, or when Adams was attacking a grizzly. Ben was once severely injured in a fight with a jaguar. He was not chained except when near a village, and then only for the safety of the excited dogs.

On one of his hunting-expeditions in the mountains of Oregon, Adams had what he considered one of the narrowest escapes of his life. He had with him as usual Rambler and Ben Franklin. While passing through a thicket Adams came unexpectedly upon a mother grizzly with cubs. The mother bear at once knocked him down and began to chew him up. Ben Franklin had not heretofore seen one of his kin.

"What will Ben do?" thought Adams, "help me or join his own kind and also attack me?"

There was neither doubt nor hesitation in Ben's

mind. Though young and small, he went to the defense of his master against a grizzly five times his own size. So vigorously did Ben throw himself upon the big grizzly that she turned from Adams and vented her fury upon Ben. Though badly wounded, Adams was able with this opportunity to reach for his rifle and kill the grizzly.

Ben ran howling to camp. Adams, also frightfully injured, followed, and found Ben lying under the wagon licking his bleeding sides. So grateful was he to Ben for saving his life that he dressed the little bear's wounds before giving attention to his own, and remained in camp several days, giving Ben every possible attention and opportunity to recover. We can understand his saying of Ben Franklin: "The most excellent of all beasts, as faithful as it is possible for any animal to be; Ben Franklin, the king of the forest, the flower of his race, my firmest friend."

The following tribute to Ben Franklin appeared in the San Francisco "Evening Bulletin" of January 19, 1858:

DEATH OF A DISTINGUISHED NATIVE CALIFORNIAN

"Ben Franklin, the grizzly bear, the favorite of the Museum man, Adams, the companion for the last three or four years of his various expeditions in the mountains and his sojourns in the cities and towns of California, departed from this mortal existence on Sunday evening, at 10 o'clock. The noble brute, which was captured at the head-waters of the Merced River in 1854, had been raised by his master from a cub, and during his life manifested the most indubitable indications of remarkable sagacity and affection. He was ever tame and gentle, and although possessed of the size and strength of a giant among brutes, was in disposition peaceful; rough it is true, in his playfulness, but always well disposed. He frequently carried his master's pack, provisions and weapons; frequently shared his blanket and fed from the same loaf.

"One of his eyes was observed to be injured and several scars were to be seen about his head and neck; but they were honorable wounds and reflected as much credit upon poor Ben as the scars of a brave soldier. They were all received in the service of his human friend, protector and master. As might be supposed his loss has been severely felt by Adams."

MISS JIM AND MR. BESSIE

During many years in the West, Mr. Philip A. Rollins was an accurate and sympathetic observer of the grizzly bear. He knew him in various localities, and saw him under countless conditions. He hunted him with a gun and then without a gun. He raised grizzlies, kindly and intelligently. He is one of the highest authorities on the grizzly. He kindly wrote for me the following from his personal experience:

"To one who knows and loves bears, Enos A. Mills, from one who loves them, Philip A. Rollins.

"One summer day, now almost thirty years ago, a cowboy, hunting from our Wyoming ranch, killed a female grizzly bear. Her two attendant cubs were brought to the ranch by the cowboy, an operation which decreased the value of his clothing, and lessened the quantity of his skin. The names of Jim and Bessie, hastily bestowed as the party, in part hauling and swearing, and in part twisting and

growling, made its arrival, were, for the sake of accuracy, later changed to Miss Jim and Mr. Bessie.

"The youngsters were presently introduced to
their sleeping quarters in the 'bear parlor,' an en-
closure connecting with the main room of the
ranch house by a doorway usually closed only with
several curtains of heavy felt. Five black bears had
their abode in the 'bear parlor' when the little grizzlies registered their advent—a registration effect-
ed by clawing and biting everybody and everything within reach. After a few days marked by
pandemonium and the enticements of very frequent meals, Miss Jim and Mr. Bessie were the
dictators of all the black bears and the friends of
all the men; of all the men, save one—he could
not refrain from teasing. Months passed; the little
grizzlies increased in strength. The teasing continued. One day a visiting surgeon set three ribs and
an arm.

"Except for this research into human anatomy,
nothing untoward happened until the end of four
years. Meanwhile the two grizzlies had, at all times,
come and gone at will into and out of the ranch
house; had, whenever they desired, tidbits sup-
plemental to their food; attended the ranch meals,
perched in orderly fashion on a bench at the
foot of the dining-table; and, after the first six
months, made any excursion they wished, being
absent from the ranch sometimes for several suc-
cessive days, going thus either alone or as the companions of whatever man might have occasion to
travel across country. These trips not infrequently
made them adjuncts of a fishing-party, and on such
occasions they were always content with their toll
of the first four fish caught—two fish for each bear.

"No attempt was ever made to exact from the bears the performance of tricks. They were treated from the outset in the same manner as one would treat a well-trained hunting hound, save that special care was taken that they should be fed before approaching either the men's dining-table in the ranch house or the lunching group of a fishing-party. On their bench at the foot of the dining-table, they never were indecorous, never snatched at any food, but would sit in dignified silence until called by name. Upon the sound of its name, the invited bear would lumber down to the floor, shuffle along to the chair of the inviter, and, having been given and somewhat gently received, the promised confection, would promptly return to its seat. It is true that the returning bear would not infrequently in passing, give playful, if vigorous, pokes into the bodies of its fellows, but none of the blows were aimed at or reached a human being.

"The grizzlies were true companions, for they had all the affectionate faithfulness of the best of dogs, intelligence far beyond that of any horse, and endless sense of humor. As to intelligence, they repeatedly used their brains in a manner which perhaps is best exemplified by the following instance of another grizzly which I watched years ago: An animal which, discovering a half-filled food-can, and prevented by the semi-closed lid from touching the contents, takes a stone between its paws and smashes the lid, has claim to brains, even if that animal be only a bear.

"I have said that nothing untoward happened during the four years. On second thought, an untoward event did occur. One November, a quantity of freshly preserved blueberries had been obtained from the East. These berries were transformed into twenty-four large deep-dish pies, one for each man on the ranch. On the date of the anticipated feast, an entertainment at a neighboring camp depopulated the house, but did not degrizzly its environs. In the early evening of that day, the house was approached by a file of men, pie-bent, expectant, joyous. Two house logs pulled from without doors, bear-tracks done upon the snow in vivid blue, forewarned that twenty-four pies had passed into history.

"At the end of the four years, Miss Jim fell victim to poison, whether set for her or for wolves we never knew. Presently Mr. Bessie was once more teased, this time by a visiting ranchman. After the ranchman had been reassembled and revived, it was decided that the bear must be done for. He should not be killed. That smacked of murder. He should not be caged in a zoölogical garden. He had not sinned according to bear law. Accordingly it was agreed that he should be lost. He was led two hundred miles from the ranch and bidden to go his way. His return to the ranch preceded that of his keeper by eight hours. He was led to the mountains of Idaho, and the duration of his return journey not improbably is still the minimum record for that course. Finally two admirers conducted him to Oregon and there parted with him forever. The last view disclosed a cheerful expression as he contemplated two hams tied to a tree, partly for purposes of strategy and partly as a parting gift."

A real acquaintance with the grizzly bear appears to fill every one with admiration for him. Mr.

William H. Wright, quoted elsewhere in this book, understood the grizzly thoroughly. His comprehensive book, "The Grizzly Bear," is dedicated with these words:

"WITH THE RESPECT, ADMIRATION AND AFFECTION
OF THE AUTHOR,
TO THE NOBLEST WILD ANIMAL OF NORTH AMERICA,
THE GRIZZLY BEAR."

New Environments

A ROCK fell from a high cliff and struck upon solid granite near a grizzly whom I was watching. There was a terrific crash and roar. Unmindful of the flying fragments and pieces bounding near, the grizzly reared up and pressed fore paws over his ears. Just as he was uncovering them the echo came thundering and booming back from a cliff across the lake. Again he hastily covered his ears with his paws to soften the ear-bursting crash.

On another occasion a wounded bear took refuge in a small thicket where the hunter was unable to get a shot at him. After failing to force the bear into the open, the hunter gave a wild, ear-splitting yell. With a growl of pain the bear at once charged furiously through the thicket toward the hunter.

A grizzly has supersensitive ears, and loud, harsh sounds give his nerves a harrowing shock. Through his higher development the grizzly probably suffers more intensely and enjoys more fully than other animals. The clashing city noises must be a never-ending irritation and torture to a bear who has been sentenced to end his days in a riotous environment. How he must yearn for the hush of the wilderness! And, as his sense of smell is also amazingly developed, perhaps he longs for a whiff of pine-spiced air and the wild, exquisite perfume of the violets.

Experience in many zoos has shown that subjecting caged grizzlies to close contact with people is usually cruelty to animals. Often they become cross, and a number of crowd-worried grizzlies have died prematurely from resultant apoplexy. Modern zoo bear-pens are constructed so that the bear is beyond the wiles of visitors—so that he can have much privacy—one of the needs of any grizzly. Perhaps we too often think of the bulky grizzly as being coarse and crude. But he is an animal of the highest type, sensitive, independent, and retiring. The normal bear is good-tempered and cheerful.

A grizzly placed in new environment in association with men will respond happily only to considerate handling and proper feeding. Tell me what a bear is fed and how, and I will tell you what the bear is—his disposition and health. A grizzly should be fed by no one except his keeper. If any one and every one feed a bear, he is likely to receive food that he ought not to eat and to have it given in a manner annoying to him. Feeding is the vital consideration for grizzly pets, for grizzlies in zoos, and for grizzlies in National Parks.

When I arrived in Colorado, in 1884, grizzlies were still common throughout the mountain areas of the State. They were numerous in a few rugged sections where there were but few people and plenty of food. In the Long's Peak region around my cabin, I early discovered the tracks of five grizzlies. One or two missing toes or some other peculiarity enabled me to determine the number. Two of these bears ranged near, and I had frequent glimpses of them.

During the autumn of one year, 1893 as I remember, I crossed the mountains between Trapper's Lake and Long's Peak. Snow covered most of the ground. During the eight days which this trip occupied I must have seen the tracks of between forty and forty-five grizzlies. I counted the tracks of eleven in one half-day. But grizzlies decreased in numbers rapidly. Numerous hunters came into the State annually. Stockmen and settlers hunted grizzlies for fun and for their hides, and professional hunters for revenue. Altogether, the grizzly had little chance for his life, and only a few survived.

In the settlement of the West many of the grizzlies had to go. Men came in with flocks of sheep and herds of cattle. The grizzlies' food was taken or driven off. Rarely did a grizzly kill any of the invading stock. Usually he worked harder for a living and took things philosophically. Many grizzlies were killed and a few sought homes elsewhere. But in the West there are still many wild regions, and in these there is room for the grizzly.

There is a wonderful unwritten story of the making of an empire—the Yellowstone—into a wildlife reservation. Big game had long been hunted in this region. The grizzly bear, since his discovery, had been relentlessly pursued; man with every conceivable contrivance was on his trail day and night; there was no quarter and no hope for peace. But suddenly firing ceased and pursuit stopped. This was epoch-marking. "What can it mean?" the grizzlies must have instantly asked. They must have asked it over and over again. But they quickly accepted it as a fact and as an advantage, and came forth to associate peacefully with man. This has made a change worth while for man. Since shooting has stopped, thousands have seen the grizzly and enjoyed him where only one saw him before.

The grizzly is easily the most popular animal in the National Parks. He really is the greatest animal on the continent. The grizzly walks: there is a dignity, a lordliness of carriage, and an indifference to all the world that impress themselves on the attention. Some one speaks quietly to him: he halts, stands on hind legs, and shows a childlike eagerness of interest in his expressive face. His attitude and responsiveness are most companionable and never fail to awake the best in every one who sees him in these moments.

Some one told me the following amusing incident concerning a grizzly. In the southwest corner of Yellowstone Park a number of boys were bathing in a stream, when a young grizzly came along and for a moment stood watching their pranks. Then he slipped quietly behind some trees upon the bank of the stream. When the boys approached this spot, with a wild "Woof, woof," he leaped into the water among them. This caused great excitement and merriment, plainly just what he desired. As he swam hurriedly away, he looked back over his shoulder with satisfaction.

Another amusing incident also happened in the Yellowstone. As the stage arrived at the Canyon Hotel, one of the passengers, who had been having much to say concerning bears, put on his raincoat and got down on all fours, proceeding to impersonate a bear. While this demonstration was on a grizzly arrived. He made a rush at the man and chased him up a tree, amid laughter and excitement. The bear made no attempt to harm any one and plainly enjoyed this prank merely as a prank.

A grizzly mother in Yellowstone Park was catching trout for her cubs one June day of 1891, when a friend and I came along. We went near to watch them. Mother grizzly charged; we fled. After one leap she stood still and appeared to be almost grinning at us. We went back, she charged, and again we ran, although she stopped at the end of the first leap. But the third time she leaped at us we stood our ground. She growled but came no nearer. Although her threats did not appear to be in earnest, we did not risk going closer; nor would I have risked standing even at that distance if we had been outside of the Park boundary.

One day I saw a bear who appeared to be suffering from a headache. A short time before he had eaten an enormous quantity of garbage. This may have been his first dinner at a garbage-pile. Standing up, he felt of his head with first one fore paw and then the other. Then, lying down, he endeavored to hold his head in both fore paws. He had just thrust it into a stream and was trying to rub it with his paw when I last saw him. On another occasion I noticed a bear suffering from a toothache. He felt of his tooth, clawed at it, and in a number of other ways showed his annoyance.

In the Yellowstone the environment of grizzlies was radically changed when it became a wild-life reservation. The numerous bear-population quickly discovered that in the Park it would not be shot at. Grizzlies at once wandered about near people with no attempt to conceal themselves and with the best of manners; there was no annoying of people, no crossness, no ferocity. This ideal association of people and grizzly bears went on unmarred for years.

Numbers of bears from far outside Park boundaries came to spend two or three months of each summer there, returning to home territory during the autumn. Other grizzlies left their homes outside the Park and moved in to stay. Whether the summer migrant bears or the recent residents came to the Park because of the food, the safety, or both is difficult to say. Unusual opportunities were furnished Park visitors to study and observe the grizzly, with beneficial influence on themselves. But their worrying of the bears in time proved harmful.

The bears were thoughtlessly betrayed. Increasing numbers of visitors produced large garbage-piles. People came to the garbage-piles to watch the bears feed and often teased them. The bears became cross. Sometimes there were fights among the assembled bears over the smelly feasts. The charity of the garbage-pile led them into bad habits, upset their digestions, and ruined their dispositions. But their appetite for garbage increased until they became food pensioners and garbage drunkards. Like some humans they enjoy being pensioners and insist on being supplied. If there wasn't enough garbage they raided camps and hotels. If their raid was interrupted they resented it. In due time a few of the most dyspeptic bears became bold and defiant raiders.

The Park is visited by thousands for whom the bears should be a source of relaxation and furnish new interests and enjoyment. But the bears are becoming unhealthy and are a menace to people. Now and then some official tries to cure the bear trouble by having a number of bears roped, tied, and whipped. Occasionally a bear is shot. There are those who advocate that the guides and officials of the Park carry guns; and still others are advocating the extermination of the grizzly. We need the grizzly. Most cures proposed are worse than his trouble. But there is a prevention in simply no garbage-piles.

In the Glacier National Park, which has been a wild-life reservation only since 1910, the grizzlies have not yet become demoralized by garbage. The grizzly bear situation in the Yellowstone is a serious and even an alarming one, and what exists here is certain to develop in other Parks. The demoralizing factors are likely to be expanded and not diminished. Then, too, in the Yellowstone this continuous eating of garbage may ere long bring on a pestilence among the grizzlies, or possibly put a check on the number of cubs born. The whole situation appears to be embraced in what I have previously said about what a grizzly is fed and how.

The grizzly has not lost all his old instincts in the Park. Around the garbage-piles he is a lazy, cross pensioner. But away from them, and especially where he ranges outside of the Park, the same bear is as alert and as energetic as ever in getting a living and watching out for his safety. They are tame near garbage-piles but a short distance away are wild. They are comparatively easy to trap near the garbage-piles, where they will enter a trap-door; but the same bear outside the Park is extremely wary and avoids going near a trap. Says William H. Wright, in "The Grizzly Bear":

"Altogether I did not find the grizzlies of Yellowstone Park in any degree more tame or less cunning than they are to-day, for example, in the Selkirks. Many of them, it is true, come to the garbage-piles to feed, but these very bears, fifty yards back in the timber, are again as wild as any of them anywhere. At the canyon, the garbage-pile is in a hollow at the foot of rather a steep incline that leads up to the edge of the woods. Bear after bear, coming down the trails that converge toward this point, will stop as he reaches the brink of this declivity, glance downward, turn his head from side to side, and launch himself down hill, with the same air of committing himself to a foreign element that one sees in the upward glance and deep breath of a man launching himself from a diving board. On their return, they invariably halted for a few seconds at the top of the hill, looked around, occasionally shook themselves, and with their first step up the familiar trail, resumed every sign of their habitual caution and alertness. While on the garbage-pile itself, they appear to pay scant attention to the people gathered behind the fairly distant wire fence, but even there, an eye familiar with their actions would note the constant watch they kept on what was going on and the hurried way in which they fed; and, fifty feet from the edge of the surrounding timber, they would at the least scent or sound or sight, bolt as incontinently as in the farthest hills. Grizzlies are no more plentiful around the Park to-day than they were twenty-five years ago in the Bitter Roots, and a hundred yards from the garbage-pile they are no different."

Apparently young bears do not inherit fear of a trap, for they are easily trapped. Young bears in captivity sometimes exhibit inherited instincts; they may be pleasurably excited with the scent of food never before seen; and they will sometimes dig down for a hidden root of a kind that their parents ate but which they themselves had never seen. In these cases of digging, they either dug at the right place from scent, or from inherited memory of place. There was nothing on the surface to indicate the presence of buried roots beneath.

The young of most animals, wild or tame, make interesting pets. But of all the pets I have known, none equal grizzly cubs for energy, alertness, and individuality. They take naturally to new, unnatural environments. A grizzly cub learns speedily and from the first tries to know everything around him. So all-knowing are his senses and his instincts that the approach of anything new at once attracts him; he stops play and with rare curiosity and concentration tries to understand it. If he solve the mystery he promptly continues play at the point where he left it.

"Baby Sylvester" is a celebrated bear story by Bret Harte that characteristically and humorously describes a bear in new environments. This little bear lost none of his native energy, alertness, and versatility under changed and unexacting conditions. The way he handled every situation was a constant surprise and delight.

Pet cubs, if gently treated, quickly accept and make the best of new environment; they become intimate and loving, in fact most intensely so. If handled kindly, the cub is willing to do everything reasonable, everything he understands one wants done. But whip or scold him, and he at once becomes stubborn and unwilling, reserved and cross. The grizzly is an animal of high type and to have him develop his best he needs fine, high consideration.

The grizzly's real character stands out when he is associated with man. He is ever true to himself. A dog will lick the hand of a cruel master or fawn on a most unworthy one. Not so the grizzly; he will not go down in the dust. Only a uniformly just man can win his loyalty or retain his friendship; he has individuality and self-respect and will not willingly serve a tyrant or even bow to him. The wearing of a hat, the holding of a pipe, the sitting up in a silly attitude, tricks which many dogs do to please a master, the grizzly will do only under compulsion. The grizzly is ever faithful and loyal to a worthy master; he will do unto you as you do unto him. Elsewhere in this book I give a number of stories which show the high character and the great possibilities of the grizzly as a companion of man if handled intelligently.

In eastern Washington, "Grizzly" Adams captured a yearling grizzly which he named Lady Washington. With her he used but little discipline, and he at all times treated her with consideration and kindness. She was constantly with him on long journeys across the mountains from State to State, in camp and on hunts. Of her Adams says:

"She has always been with me; and often shared my dangers and privations, borne my burdens, and partaken of my meals. The reader may be surprised to hear of a grizzly companion and friend, but Lady Washington has been both to me. He may hardly credit the accounts of my nestling up between her and the fire to keep both sides warm under the frosty skies of the mountains, but all this is true."

The ability to comprehend a new situation or incident and readjust one's self to it is the act of an open and a thinking mind. The food, religion, politics, and personal habits of an individual are changed slowly and with difficulty. Progress is constantly being held back by old customs—the inability of the race to form new habits meeting new conditions. Many species of extinct animals have perished because of over-specialization. "Leave your prejudice at home" was the best advice I received just prior to a trip to Europe. Prejudice and its allied mental conditions are binding and delaying. The grizzly does not allow old prejudice to prevent his exploring for new information, and he is ever ready for something new in his environment.

In a generation or two the grizzly has become

expert in eluding the pursuer; he rivals the fox in concealing his trail, in confounding the trailer and escaping with his life. That he has developed this trait since coming in contact with the white man and the repeating rifle—out of necessity—there can be no doubt. Formerly, the rightful monarch of the wilds through superiority, he roamed freely about, indifferent as to where he went or whether or not he was seen. He has been wise enough to readjust himself to the evolutionary and revolutionary forces introduced by man. The king of the wilderness has survived through retreat; he has become the master of strategy. Instinct hardly accounts for this swift evolution. The readjustment—avoiding man—does not indicate cowardice; it indicates brains. In the warfare of existence, in changing, exacting environments, the grizzly bear has risen triumphant.

Description, History, and Classification

BEARS appear to be of Old World origin. Fossils tell of their existence in Asia eons ago. The first bear emigrants perhaps landed in Alaska more than a million years ago. They may have come over on one of the land bridges which have at times connected Asia and America.

"In the Old World, bears were first distinguishable in the Upper Miocene, and may there be traced back to forms which were unmistakably derivatives of the early dogs," says Mr. William B. Scott in "A History of Land Mammals in the Western Hemisphere."

It is interesting that bears, dogs, and seals descended from a common ancestor. Seals have been called "sea bears." The bear lives for a long period each year without either food or drink. During this period he lies dormant. The seal has the habit of doing without food and drink and also sleep for weeks while leading an active life. The bear and the dog are alike in many ways. Both accept domestication readily and both become loyal and intimate associates of man. Many of their ways in play are alike, and each has the habit of sometimes becoming restless in his home locality and traveling afar for adventure.

In North America bears have branched out into numerous species, and here they have attained their greatest development. South America has, perhaps, only one small species, and Africa only one. Europe and Asia combined are accredited with having eight species.

The grizzly is distributed over the western half of North America, from northern Alaska far down into Mexico. His home is more generally in the mountains. He is also found in the barren lands of Canada, in the Bad Lands of the Upper Missouri, and in the western margin of the Great Plains. On a number of the wilderness islands of the Alaskan and Northwest Coast, where he is of unusually large size, he forms a numerous population.

The similarity of the mental processes and the customs of the various species of Alaskan bears has been remarked upon by many people. Mr. Charles Sheldon, the hunter-scientist, says:

"Nothing is more striking than the general similarity in nature, actions, appearance, and habits of both the brown bears of the humid coast region of Alaska and the grizzlies of the dry interior. The several species of both the coast and inland bears differ more or less widely in size, anatomy, color, and claws, but no one can observe them in their natural habitats without realizing that all have descended from a common ancestor."

The little that I have seen of the polar bear suggests to me that he may be related to the grizzly. It is interesting that the coats of the polar bear are uniformly white, while those of the grizzly are of assorted colors.

The grizzly is scattered over a vast and varied range, feeds on a variety of food, and is divided into numerous species and subspecies, but he ever runs true to character, everywhere is one hundred per cent grizzly. The chief points of dissimilarity in the different species are the shape of the skull and the character of the teeth. Rarely is there any difference apparent in the living animals; the classification is determined chiefly from the teeth and the formation of the skull.

Color is no clue to the species. Color may vary as much in one species, or even in one litter of cubs, as in different species widely separated as to locality. Assemble a number of grizzlies representing each of the many species and subspecies, and there will be a bewildering array of fur coats, perhaps no two alike. However, as I have said, the grizzly's characteristics are ever the same, no matter what the color of his coat or where he lives. Wherever you see a grizzly—on the glaciers of Alaska, on the desert sands of Mexico, or fishing in the Columbia—he seems as much the same old acquaintance as the bluebird who comes each spring.

The color of the species runs through many shades of brown: among them are cream, tan, mouse-color, cinnamon, and golden yellow. Black or almost white may be the fur of the grizzly, but shades of gray and brown predominate. Infrequently a grizzly is seen with a coat of more than one color. This variety of color causes confusion concerning species, but within the bounds of the United States, outside of Alaska, there are virtually only two kinds of bear, the black and the grizzly, though these are divided by naturalists into many species and subspecies according to the arrangement and forms of their teeth and the bones of the head. Cinnamon and brown are common colors of both grizzlies and black bears.

The fur of the grizzly, like any fur, is composed of a fine, thick fleece lining and long, coarse hairs which project from it. The under fur may be of any color, but the hairs that project through this are, I believe, invariably dark with a silver tip.

Commonly the fur is long and shaggy on the grizzly's flanks and shoulders.

The grizzly is from six to seven feet long and in contour is pointed in front, and heavy, though well-rounded, behind. His shoulders are high. The body of the grizzly is longer, straighter along the back line, and less humped on the haunches than the black bear's. The grizzly's head is narrower, the jaws and nose longer and less blunt, than the black's.

The grizzly always appears larger than he really is. The average weight is between three hundred and fifty and six hundred pounds; males weigh a fourth more than females. Few grizzlies weigh more than seven hundred pounds, though exceptional specimens are known to have weighed more than one thousand. Adams gave the weight of "Samson," a California grizzly, as fifteen hundred pounds, and a few Alaskan grizzlies, judging by their skins, may have weighed more than "Samson." It may be that years ago, when not so closely hunted, the grizzly lived longer and grew to a larger size than he attains to-day.

The grizzly looks capable and substantial. His massive proportions suggest strength rather than bulk. With back broad and well-rounded, and feet pulled well together beneath him, he may at first appearance seem top-heavy. But this impression is forgotten the instant his movements display his ease of adjustment and nicety of balance. Without effort he raises himself on hind legs to his full height gracefully and stands with the repose of a statue.

Many of his movements appear awkward and clumsy. He is loose-jointed and sometimes is rather lumbering; he often shuffles as though wearing a large, loose wooden shoe on each foot. Commonly he travels along with a gait neither walk nor trot. Yet the bear is exceedingly speedy and few horses can overtake him. His endurance is astounding.

He has extraordinary strength. I have known him to drag the carcass of a cow or a steer of twice his own weight. In several instances this was dragged up the mountain-side over fallen logs, yet it was apparently moved without extraordinary effort.

The grizzly is exceptionally expert and agile with his paws. With either fore paw he can strike like a sledge-hammer or lift a heavy weight. He boxes or strikes with lightning-like rapidity. Most grizzlies are right-handed; that is, the right fore paw is most used. If a small object is to be touched or moved, he will daintily use but one claw. The black bear would use the entire paw.

The fore-foot prints made by the grizzly are much shorter than the tracks made by his hind feet. His hind foot leaves a track similar to the bare-footed track of a man, while the track of the fore foot has the appearance of the grizzly's having walked upon the front of his foot—the ball and toes—with the heel upraised. The fore claws are from two to five inches long, the hind claws much shorter.

The fore ankles of the grizzly are smaller than the black bear's, the hind feet relatively larger; the claws are much longer and less curved. The grizzly's claws do not curve as sharply downward as a black's, but the claw-points extend well beyond the ends of the toes. The black's curved claws are much used in climbing; the grizzly's claws are used mostly for digging.

The largest grizzly-track that I have measured was slightly more than thirteen inches long, and seven and one half inches wide at the widest point. These measurements did not include the clawmarks. In places where this bear had slipped on snowy or muddy ground the track with clawmarks was of most formidable appearance. Many of the big Alaskan grizzlies have large feet, sometimes making a track eighteen inches in length. However, in the Rocky Mountains I have seen a large track that had been made by a comparatively small bear. More than once I have seen bears weighing less than four hundred pounds whose feet were larger than those of other bears who weighed upwards of six hundred pounds. A large grizzly bear track does not necessarily indicate that it is the track of a large bear.

There is marked difference in the ordinary ways of the black and the grizzly. The grizzly is energetic, thorough, works hard, and takes life rather seriously; while the black bear is lazy, careless, does no more work each day than is necessary, and is more playful. The grizzly's hibernating-den is usually a substantial, complete affair, while that of the black bear is more or less of a makeshift. The black bear likes to play with other bears, while the grizzly enjoys playing alone. The black climbs a tree easily and often sleeps in a tree-top; the grizzly bear rarely climbs after he passes cubhood.

Most of the time the grizzly is silent. When he does say anything it is in a queer, but expressive, language. He utters a choppy champ of a cough; he says "Woof," "Woof," with various accents; he growls eloquently; he grunts and he sniffs. The youngsters say something like "Eu-wow-wow," and when forlorn give an appealing cry I cannot translate into words.

Little is known concerning the mating-habits of

wild grizzly bears. The majority of authorities maintain that mating takes place in June and July, while a few believe that it occurs late in the autumn. The few times that I have seen males and females together were in late June and July.

Although known to the white race only a little more than a century, the grizzly has been a part of the life and legends of the Indians for countless generations. Often feared, frequently admired, his brain and brawn are featured again and again; he is always the acknowledged chief and master of the wilderness.

Many are the names that he carries: grizzly bear, silver-tip, white bear, bald-face, cinnamon bear, roach-back, range bear, and others.

The first printed mention of the grizzly that I know of is one by Edward Umfreville, who, in writing concerning Hudson's Bay in 1790, mentions the "Grizzle Bear." In 1795 Sir Alexander MacKenzie writes of the "Grisly Bear." But the grizzly was given a definite place in history when Lewis and Clark mentioned him in their Journal, in April, 1805, as the "white bear." Much that they wrote was made public, and the bear's career started, by Governor DeWitt Clinton in an address before the Literary and Philosophical Society of New York, May 4, 1814.

As is shown by Guthrie's Geography, George Ord, the naturalist, described and first classified the grizzly as *Ursus horribilis*, in 1815. This was from information which Brackenridge had gathered, chiefly from the Journal of Lewis and Clark, and was based on the "white bear" of the type locality of the Missouri River a little above the mouth of Poplar River, northeastern Montana.

Dr. C. Hart Merriam is the supreme authority

concerning bears. Following I give his classification of the grizzly and big brown bears, together with quotations from his introduction to "North American Fauna, No. 41" (1918):

REVIEW OF THE GRIZZLY AND BIG BROWN BEARS
OF NORTH AMERICA (*Genus Ursus*)
"WITH DESCRIPTION OF A NEW GENUS
VETULARCTOS ·

"When Audubon and Bachman published their great work on the Mammals of North America (1846–1854), and in fact up to the year 1857, it was commonly believed by naturalists as well as by hunters and the public generally that there was only a single species of grizzly bear—the one described by Lewis and Clark in 1804–5, and named *Ursus horribilis* by Ord in 1815. Baird, in 1857, described another species, from Coppermines, New Mexico, which he named *Ursus horriæus*.

"Nearly forty years later, in my 'Preliminary Synopsis of the American Bears,' eight grizzlies and big brown bears were recognized, of which five were described as new. It was not then suspected that the number remaining to be discovered was anything like so great as has since proved to be the case. The steady influx of specimens resulting from the labors of the Biological Survey, supplemented by the personal efforts of a number of hunter-naturalists, brought to light many surprises, most of which have been published; and beginning in the spring of 1910, a fund placed at my disposal made it possible to offer hunters and trappers sufficient inducement to tempt them to exert themselves in securing needed specimens. As a result, the national collection of bears has steadily grown until, in number of species represented, in completeness of series, and in number of type specimens, it now far excels all other collections in the world together.

"Nevertheless there are many gaps in the series. Knowledge of the big bears is by no means complete and many years must pass before the last word on the subject will be written. Many bears now roaming the wilds will have to be killed and their skulls and skins sent to museums before their characters and variations will be fully understood and before it will be possible to construct accurate maps of their ranges. Persons having the means and ambition to hunt big game may be assured that bears are still common in many parts of British Columbia, Yukon Territory, and Alaska, and that much additional material is absolutely required to settle questions still in doubt. . . .

"Some writers have advanced the view that the various species of bears freely interbreed. Let those so minded ask themselves the question, If promiscuous interbreeding were to take place, what would become of the species? From the nature of the case, the stability of species depends on the rarity of crossings with other species, for if interbreeding were to take place frequently the species so interbreeding would of course cease to exist, having merged into a common hybrid. Hybrids now and then occur, particularly in zoölogical gardens, but among wild animals in their native haunts they are exceedingly rare.

"The number of species here given will appear to many as preposterous. To all such I extend a cordial invitation to visit the National Museum and see for themselves what the bear skulls show. Recognition of species is a matter of interpretation. If the material is adequate there can be little room for difference of opinion; if inadequate, many important points must remain in doubt. It is not the business of the naturalist either to create or to suppress species, but to endeavor to ascertain how many Nature has established, and having discovered this, to point out their characters and learn as much as possible about them.

"One of the unlooked-for results of the critical study of the American bears is the discovery that the big bears, like mice and other small mammals, split up into a large number of forms whose ranges in some cases overlap so that three or more species may be found in the same region.

"Another surprising result is the discovery that Admiralty Island in Southwestern Alaska appears to be inhabited by no less than five distinct species, each of which is obviously related to and representative of an adjacent mainland species. ...

SEXUAL DIFFERENCES

"In most species of bears the males are much larger than the females. In some the disparity in size is very remarkable, as in *middendorffi* of Kodiak Island and *magister* of southern California. In a few cases the difference is slight, as in *kidderi* of Alaska Peninsula.

AGE DIFFERENCES

"Bear skulls undergo a series of changes from early life to old age, and in most species do not attain their mature form until seven or more years of age. In species having the frontal shield highly elevated, as in *middendorffi, kluane, stikeenensis,* and *mirabilis,* the frontals reach their maximum of arching or bulging in early adult life (about the sixth year), after which they gradually become flatter. . . .

CLASSIFICATION OF GRIZZLY AND BIG BROWN BEARS

"The differences formerly supposed to exist between the grizzlies and the big brown bears appear, in the light of the material now available, to distinguish certain groups of species from certain other groups, rather than the grizzlies collectively from the big brown bears collectively. In other words, the differences between the grizzlies on the one hand and the big brown bears on the other are neither so great nor so constant as at one time believed. And there are species which in the present state of knowledge cannot be positively referred to either group. In fact, it seems at least possible that certain species which appear to belong with the grizzlies are closely related to certain other species which clearly belong with the big brown bears. The typical brown bears differ from the typical grizzlies in peculiarities of color, claws, skull, and teeth. The color of the former is more uniform, with less of the surface grizzling due to admixture of pale-tipped hairs; the claws are shorter, more curved, darker, and scurfy instead of smooth; the skull is more massive; the fourth lower premolar is conical, lacking the sulcate heel of the true grizzlies. But these are average differences, not one of which holds true throughout the group. Most of the specimens in museums consist of skulls only, unaccompanied by skins or claws, leaving a doubt as to the external characters; and in old bears the important fourth lower premolar is likely to be so worn that its original form cannot be made out. And, worst of all, some of the grizzlies lack the distinctive type of premolar, leaving only the skull as a guide to their affinities. The present classification, therefore, must be regarded as tentative and subject to revision. ...

"The present paper is merely a review of the existing state of knowledge of the grizzlies and big brown bears of America and does not include either the polar or the black bears. It is not intended as a monographic revision, but aims to supply a list of the species, together with descriptions and comparisons of adult skulls, chiefly males. Little is said of external characters, for the reason that little is known, only a few skins with claws being available for study.

LIST OF SPECIES AND SUBSPECIES OF GRIZZLY AND
BIG BROWN BEARS, WITH TYPE LOCALITIES.[1]

(*Classification provisional.*)

Horribilis group:
  Ursus horribilis horribi-
      lis Ord ....Missouri River, northeastern Montana.
    horribilis bairdi Mer-
        riam ....Blue River, Summit County, Colorado.
  horribilisimperator
      Merriam ....Yellowstone National Park, Wyoming.
    chelidonias nobis ...Jervis Inlet, British Columbia.

---

[1] "Nearly 130 years ago Prof. Zauschner proposed the name *Ursus saribur* for an animal 'from the region of Canada' (Bestimmung der Hundsart Krokute, und der Bärenart Saribur, p. 8, 1788), but the species appears to be impossible of identification."

atnarko nobis ......Atnarko River, British Columbia.

kwakiutl Merriam ..Jervis Inlet, British Columbia.

nortoni Merriam ...Southeastern side Yakutat Bay, Alaska.

warburtoni Merriam.Atnarko River, British Columbia.

neglectus Merriam ..Near Hawk Inlet, Admiralty Island, Southeastern Alaska.

californicus Merriam.Monterey, California.

tularensis Merriam..Fort Tejon, California.

colusus Merriam....Sacramento Valley, California.

dusorgus nobis[1].....Jack Pine River, Alberta-British Columbia boundary.

Planiceps group:

Ursus nelsoni Merriam.Colonia Garcia, Chihuahua, Mexico.

texensis texensis Merriam ....Davis Mountains, Texas.

texensis navaho Merriam ....Navajo country near Fort Defiance, Arizona. (Probably Chuska Mts.)

planiceps nobis.....Colorado (exact locality uncertain).

macrodon nobis.....Twin Lakes, Colorado.

mirus nobis........Yellowstone National Park, Wyoming.

eltonclarki Merriam.Near Freshwater Bay, Chichagof Island, Alaska.

tahltanicus Merriam.Klappan Creek (= Third South Fork Stikine River), British Columbia.

insularis Merriam...Admiralty Island, Alaska.

orgilos Merriam.....Bartlett Bay, east side Glacier Bay, Southeastern Alaska.

---

[1] "Reference to group provisional."

orgiloides nobis..... Italio River, Alaska.

pallasi Merriam..... Donjek River, southwestern Yukon.

rungiusi rungiusi nobis .... Rocky Mountains, headwaters Athabaska River, Alberta.

rungiusi sagittalis nobis .... Champagne Landing, southwestern Yukon.

macfarlani nobis.... Anderson River, 50 miles below Fort Anderson, Mackenzie.

canadensis Merriam[1].Moose Pass, near Mount Robson, British Columbia.

Arizonæ group:
Ursus arizonæ Merriam.............. Escudilla Mts., Apache County, Arizona.

idahoensis nobis.... North Fork Teton River, eastern Idaho.

pulchellus pulchellus nobis .... Ross River, Yukon.

pulchellus ereunetes nobis .... Beaverfoot Range, Kootenay District, British Columbia.

oribasus nobis...... Upper Liard River, Yukon.

chelan Merriam..... East slope Cascade Mts., Chelan County, Washington.

shoshone Merriam... Estes Park, Colorado.

kennerlyi Merriam.. Mountains of northeastern Sonora, near Los Nogales, Mexico.

utahensis Merriam.. Salina Creek, near Mayfield, Utah.

perturbans nobis.... Mount Taylor, northern New Mexico.

---

[1] "Reference to group provisional."

rogersi rogersi nobis . Upper Greybull River, Absaroka Mountains, Wyoming.

rogersi bisonophagus
nobis . . . . Black Hills (Bear Lodge), northeastern Wyoming.

pervagor Merriam . . . Pemberton Lake (now Lillooet Lake), British Columbia.

caurinus Merriam . . . Berners Bay, east side Lynn Canal, Southeastern Alaska.

eulophus Merriam . . . Admiralty Island, Southeastern Alaska.

klamathensis Merriam[1] . . . . Beswick, near mouth Shovel Creek, Klamath River, northern California.

mendocinensis Merriam[1] . . . . Long Valley, Mendocino County, California.

magister Merriam[1] . . Los Biacitos, Santa Ana Mountains, Southern California.

Hylodromus group:

Ursus hylodromus Elliot . . . . Rocky Mountains, western Alberta.

kluane kluane Merriam . . . . McConnell River, Yukon.

kluane impiger nobis . Columbia Valley, British Columbia.

pellyensis nobis . . . . . Ketza Divide, Pelly Mountains, Yukon.

andersoni nobis[1] . . . . Dease River, near Great Bear Lake, Mackenzie.

---

[1] "Reference to group provisional."

Horriæus group:

> *Ursus apache* Merriam . Whorton Creek, south slope White Mts., eastern Arizona (a few miles west of Blue).

>> *horriæus* Baird . . . . . Coppermines, southwestern New Mexico.

>> *henshawi* Merriam . . Southern Sierra Nevada, near Havilah, Kern County, California.

Stikeenensis group:

> *Ursus stikeenensis* Merriam . . . . Tatletuey Lake, tributary to Finlay River, near head Skeena River, British Columbia.

>> *crassodon* nobis . . . . . Klappan Creek (= Third South Fork Stikine River), British Columbia.

>> *crassus* nobis[1] . . . . . . Upper Macmillan River, Yukon.

>> *mirabilis* Merriam[1] . . Admiralty Island, Alaska.

>> *absarokus* Merriam[1] . Little Bighorn River, northern Bighorn Mountains, Montana.

Alascensis group:

> *Ursus alascensis* Merriam . . . . Unalaklik River, Alaska.

>> *toklat* Merriam . . . . . Head of Toklat River, north base Alaska Range, near Mount McKinley, Alaska.

>> *latifrons* Merriam . . . Jasper House, Alberta.

Richardsoni group:

> *Ursus richardsoni* Swainson . . . . Shore of Arctic Ocean, west side Bathurst Inlet, near mouth of Hood River.

---

[1] "Reference to group provisional."

russelli Merriam[1]... West side Mackenzie River delta, Canada.

phæonyx Merriam[1].. Glacier Mountain, Tanana Mts., Alaska (about 2 miles below source of Comet Creek, near Forty-mile Creek, between Yukon and Tanana Rivers).

internationalis Merriam .... Alaska-Yukon boundary, about 50 miles south of Arctic coast.

ophrus Merriam.... Eastern British Columbia (exact locality unknown).

washake Merriam... North Fork Shoshone River, Absaroka Mts., western Wyoming.

Kidderi group:
Ursus kidderi kidderi
Merriam .... Chinitna Bay, Cook Inlet, Alaska.
kidderi tundrensis
Merriam .... Shaktolik River, Norton Sound, Alaska.
eximius Merriam.... Head of Knik Arm, Cook Inlet, Alaska.

Innuitus group:
Ursus innuitus Merriam .... Golofnin Bay, south side Seward Peninsula, northwestern Alaska.

cressonus Merriam.. Lakina River, south slope Wrangell Range, Alaska.

alexandræ Merriam[1]. Kusilof Lake, Kenai Peninsula, Alaska.

---

[1] "Reference to group provisional."

Townsendi group:
    Ursus townsendi Merri-
        am ....Mainland of Southeastern
                      Alaska (exact locality
                      uncertain).

Dalli group:
    Ursus dalli Merriam...Yakutat Bay (northwest
                      side), Alaska.
      hoots Merriam......Clearwater Creek, a north
                      branch of Stikine River,
                      British Columbia.
      sitkensis Merriam...Sitka Islands, Alaska.
      shirasi Merriam.....Pybus Bay, Admiralty Is-
                      land, Alaska.
      nuchek Merriam[1]...Head of Nuchek Bay, Hin-
                      chinbrook Island, Prince
                      William Sound, Alaska.

Gyas group:
    Ursus gyas Merriam...Pavlof Bay, Alaska Penin-
                      sula.
      middendorffi Mer-
        riam ....Kodiak Island, Alaska.

Kenaiensis group:
    Ursus kenaiensis Merri-
        am ....Cape Elizabeth, extreme
                      west end Kenai Penin-
                      sula, Alaska.
      sheldoni Merriam...Montague Island, Prince
                      William Sound, Alaska.

Vetularctos genus nobis (pp. 131–133, 'North Amer-
    ican Fauna, No. 41'):
    Vetularctos inopinatus
        nobis ....Rendezvous Lake, north-
                      east of Fort Anderson,
                      Mackenzie.

---

[1] "Reference to group provisional."

Will the Grizzly be Exterminated?

THE grizzly bear is vanishing so rapidly that without protection he is likely to become extinct. If there is good reason—and there is—for the protection of deer, elk, and the bighorn, there is every good reason why we should protect the grizzly. He is a destroyer of pests, he helps sustain a hunting-industry, he encourages many individuals to take mental relaxation and healthful exercise in the outdoors, he carries more popular and sustained interest than any other animal, and, in most respects, he is the greatest wild animal in the world. It will benefit the human race to perpetuate the grizzly, and to do this will require a few years of legal protection.

A close season for a period of years is needed. If there is an open season this should be restricted to two or three States, and it should be short. The number taken should be limited to one per person, unless a mother grizzly with cubs be killed, in which case the cubs also may be captured. The use of steel trap, deadfall, poison, spring gun, and dogs should be prohibited and the sale of hides forbidden.

Most big game has had some protection for years; the grizzly has had none. He is not a bad fellow, there is no just claim against him, but he has paid the penalty of being misunderstood. He has been classed as a menace and relentlessly pursued as though a dangerous criminal. Men follow him the year round, with guns, dogs, horses, traps, and poison. He is even trailed to the hibernating-den and slaughtered without any chance for his life.

Fear of bears and prejudice against them is all too often taught and developed in childhood. Mothers and nurses hush children by telling them, "Bears will get you if you're not good." People, however, are now learning that bears are not ferocious, that they do not eat human flesh, and that in the wilds the grizzly flees from man as though from a pestilence.

Mr. Pocock, in "A Man in the Open," with quaint, satirical philosophy goes to the bottom of the grizzly question. He says:

"The coarse treatment grizzlies gets from hunters makes them sort of bashful with any stranger. Ye see, b'ars yearns to man, same as the heathen does to their fool gods, whereas bullets, pizen, and deadfalls is sort of discouraging. Their sentiments gets mixed, they acts confused and naturally if they're shot at they'll get hostile, same as you and me. They is misunderstood and that's how nobody has a kind word for grizzlies."

Grizzlies are walking mouse-traps. They are, like birds, destroyers of pests, and give us services of economic value. They are useful for what they eat; their food is made up in part of mice, rats, rabbits, ants, grasshoppers, and stray carcasses, and the remainder may be considered of little or no value to man.

A grizzly came down into a rancher's meadow in southern Colorado and "rooted it up like a hog." The owner was up in arms and one morning killed the invader. Curious as to what the grizzly could have been eating, he sent for a local butcher. His "insides" showed, among other things, the remains of thirty-four mice, one rat, and one rabbit.

Rarely does a grizzly kill cattle. This killing, when done, is by one grizzly. Perhaps ninety-nine out of every hundred grizzlies never kill any stock or big game. Then, too, when a grizzly kills cattle he usually makes a business of it, and if one should get the habit he could be specially disposed of. Protection to the grizzly would not be at the expense of live stock or big game.

During rambles in the mountains through the years I have investigated more than fourteen cases in which the grizzly was charged with killing cattle. In a number of instances there was not a trace of a grizzly near the carcass. There were traces of other animals, but the guilty one could not be determined. There were eleven carcasses that had been visited by grizzlies; six of these animals had been killed by lions, one by poisonous plants, one by wolves, two by stones that rolled from a landslip. In the eleventh case neither the carcass nor its surroundings gave any conclusive evidence for determining the cause of the cow's death. The carcass had been fed upon by coyotes, wolves, lions and both black and grizzly bears. But what killed the cow? It might have been lightning or disease, a wolf or a lion, or possibly a hunter. Many hunters are not up on natural history and shoot at the first object that moves. The only evidence against the grizzly was entirely circumstantial; he had eaten a part of the carcass.

The killing of wild life is not in my line. I am not a hunter. But in the hunting-industry the grizzly heads the list. The hunter will pay more for a shot at a grizzly than for a shot at any other, and often all other, big game. Hunters frequently spend from one thousand to many thousands of dollars in going after the grizzly. They will work harder and longer for a grizzly than for any other animal.

But the grizzly-hunting industry is coming to an end through decreasing numbers of grizzlies. A short time ago the "Saturday Evening Post" said: "The betting is a thousand to one that you will never kill a grizzly inside the United States. There are a few left but not many; and all are highly trained in suspiciousness and resourcefulness."

If the hunting of grizzlies is to continue, the grizzly must promptly have some protection. Mr. J.A. McGuire, editor of "Outdoor Life," has been working for years to bring about legal protection and intelligent understanding of bears. At last it looks as though he would succeed. But much work is yet to be done before all States give bears proper protection, before bear natural histories are rewritten and bears are appreciated at their real, their high, worth. Writing is a hunter-naturalist, Mr. McGuire says:

"When the grizzly bear shall have passed—and he is found in such lamentably small numbers now that his exit from our midst is but a question of years—there shall have disappeared from our mountains one of the sublimest specimens of animal life that exalts the western wilderness. As a sporting trophy, his hide stands at the top of the list of American wild animals—one which sportsmen from all over the world have come here to secure. Nowhere else in the world can the grizzly bear be found except in western North America, and we as sportsmen naturalists should see to it that his demise is not hastened and that his life shall be preserved to posterity."

Shooting is not all there is to hunting. Hunters while hunting often take on a new lease of effi-

ciency, even though they do not get the grizzly.
Often, too, they make the intimate acquaintance of
another hunter, or of a guide, and return with en-
larged views into human nature; or they develop a
new and worth-while outdoor interest. So that, considered solely for hunting purposes, the grizzly has
both a commercial and a higher value.

Any one who sees a grizzly bear in his rugged
mountain home or even in a National Park, which
is a wilderness-land, will receive a lasting impression. It is the character of this animal that stands
out. He is of heroic size and powerfully built, but
he is at all times so dignified, and so wide-awake,
that his individuality never fails to impress you.
The splendid animal and the scene wherein he
stood will often be recalled. Again and again you
will wonder concerning him and his life, his neighbors, and his territory. The interest which you have
received may lead you to revisit the wild, revivify-
ing mountain-land in which he lives.

When the hunter ceased firing in the Yellowstone National Park, the grizzly bear was the first
of the big wild animals to discover that it was safe
to show himself. The wildest animal, extremely shy
of being seen even at long range, he showed his superior intelligence, his strong character, in being
the first to realize that times had changed and that
man had ceased trying to kill the wild folks on
sight. It took the other big animals a long time to
learn that they were protected. Many of them re-
lied on old experiences, and for years, on the approach of man, they ran for their lives.

National Parks are developing a friendly interest
in grizzlies, and there is a growing appreciation of
the grizzly's true worth. But just at present this appreciation and this sentiment are not strong

enough to protect the grizzly without the formal assistance of a grizzly-protection law.

During the past twenty-five years the grizzly population has enormously decreased. The grizzly is in danger of extermination. In California, where he was once numerous, he is now extinct. He has also gone from extensive areas in all the other Western States. In the areas where he still exists the population is in most places sparse.

It is doubtful if he is holding his own anywhere within the bounds of the United States, unless it be in Glacier National Park. The grizzly population of the Yellowstone National Park is variously estimated from fifty to one hundred. But each year numbers of cubs born inside the Park are trapped just outside of it, and old bears whose home is inside the Park are occasionally shot outside the boundary-line. It may be that the bears coming in from outside, a few of whom each year appear to move into the Park to live, may maintain the normal or possibly slightly increase the population; but this is doubtful. There are a few grizzlies in the Rocky Mountain National Park, perhaps a few in the Mount Rainier Park, and a number in four or five of the Canadian National Parks. Alaska is the grizzly country at present; but dozens of hunters are each year putting a check on its increase in grizzly population, except in the Mount McKinley National Park.

The grizzly needs protection at once, needs your active interest now. He is making his last stand and is surrounded by relentless foes. Protection only will save him and enable him to perpetuate himself. Without the grizzly the wilds would be dull, the canyon and the crag would lose their eloquent appeal. This wild uncrowned king has won his place in nature which no other animal can fill. We need the grizzly bear—the King of the Wilderness World.

With a closed season everywhere in the United States for a few years, the bears would increase in numbers and in due time areas now depopulated would be again peopled by them. Among the grizzlies there are always adventurers who wander far away looking for new scenes. These exploring grizzlies, as numbers increased, might redistribute themselves. Grizzlies in western Oregon might wander southward and even restock the four National Parks of California, where there is now not a grizzly. But this would require a cessation of the shooting of grizzlies for a number of years.

The population might be more quickly affected by restocking. A few grizzlies could be trapped in Yellowstone and set free in these other National Parks. The problem of restocking unoccupied areas would not be difficult if there could be for a few years a general closed season. In restocking these areas the zoos could not help. So far grizzlies have not been successfully bred in confinement.

The grizzly is an educational factor of enormous potential value. An acquaintance with him will give a lively interest in the whole world of nature, in both natural history and the natural resources of the earth. A knowledge of these will increase the enjoyment and the usefulness of every one.

In learning natural history the grizzly might well be the first life studied. Interest in him could be used to arouse interest in all life. In the very beginnings of interest in any living thing there is a desire for information concerning its food. Soil, directly or indirectly, produces the entire food-supply of the earth. Thus the trail of the grizzly bear would lead one to the wonderful story of soil-creation and the strange, almost enchanting powers it has over our strange existence.

For the young, and perhaps for the older, the grizzly has qualities which should make him the supreme mental stimulus of the great outdoors. A better acquaintance with him will be beneficial of itself, and an interest in him would inevitably extend to his wild neighbors and to the whole wide world of beauty and grandeur wherein he lives his adventurous life.

The eagle, our emblematic bird, has prowess; he soars, he dares the storm, and he explores the cloud scenery of the sky. He makes an appeal to the interest of a few, but the bear stirs the minds and the hearts of many. In most respects the grizzly would rival the eagle for an emblematic animal and would excel all animals in arousing a nature interest around the world.

Perpetuate the grizzly in our wild places and National Parks, and this will fill all wild scenes again with their appealing primeval spell—the master touch which stirs the imagination. An educator has called the imagination "the supreme intellectual faculty"; it is creative, original, refreshing. The imagination will be alive so long as the grizzly lives.

In art alone the grizzly is a subject worthy of the sculptor. He will help quicken and develop the creative imagination of any one who knows him—the grizzly of heroic art.

The grizzly probably heads the animal list in brain-power. He is still developing. He appreciates play and he has marked individuality. He is the greatest animal that is without a voice. Stories of "this animal that walks like man" ever appeal; he is the most impressive animal on the continent. He is the dominant and the most distinguished animal of the world.

AFTERWORD

RAY L. GROSVENOR

Threatened by extinction, the grizzly is making a last stand against the encroachment of man. His back is up against the wall. From 1968 to 1972 in Yellowstone there were 33 grizzlies reluctantly shot by rangers in the interests of the public safety. There was some comparative safety for the big bear while there was still some wilderness left for this huge and solitary animal. The explosion of people able and equipped to pack into the wilderness since the end of World War II seriously threatens the survival of this magnificent mammal.

It would be especially distressing to Enos A. Mills to learn that the grizzly is no longer to be found at all in Colorado today. There are now between only 500 and 1,000 of these magnificent bears left in the entire United States, mostly in Yellowstone National Park and in Glacier National Park.

Ursus arctos horribilis! That is the scientific name for what is commonly called the "Grizzly Bear." The first and second names mean "bear" in Latin and Greek. You don't have to be a classics scholar to understand the third and final part of the name.

The prejudice goes back in time. One encounter Lewis and Clark had with Indians along the Columbia River is an interesting comment on the reputation of the grizzly among the natives of that region. The explorers had collected a number of pelts on their long journey and found that the Indians clearly distinguished between *hohhost* (the grizzly) and *yakah* (the common brown bear). The color ranges of the grizzly run from silver to charcoal to very dark brown. The Indians warned the members of the expedition against confusing one of the many shades of the grizzly with that of the less ferocious brown bear, and trying to track or kill the grizzly. The Indians were also among the first to claim that the grizzly could not climb trees. Weighing, as they do, from a quarter of a ton to half a ton, there are undeniably many trees that they would not care to climb. But we have learned that grizzlies do indeed climb trees. Ask the man who, in a well-documented case, was chased by a grizzly not up one but two trees in succession in Glacier National Park in 1968, the year following the double tragedy there. He has lived to tell the story and has the scars to back up his claim.

The terrible legends of the grizzly flowed eastward during the explorations of the 19th century, yet he captured the imagination and, more, the respect of the mountain men, the hunters and scouts of that era. One such trapper, James Adams, managed to tame three grizzly cubs in the 1850's. Two of them survived a trip around the Horn to be displayed in the east by Barnum. Even here legends grew and these two caged bears, after being raised free of any chain or containment, are supposed to have grabbed monkeys in the show and torn them to bits, devouring them for the especial benefit of the public. True or not, the stories did not harm the box office receipts.

Bad press has continued until today, despite the fact that at Yellowstone National Park there have been only two deaths reported from grizzlies in the period of over a hundred years since the establishment of the park in 1872. Indeed, more people have been seriously injured (and some have died) from falling into the thermal pools than have suffered anything more than fright plus a good deal of excitement from any contact with grizzlies.

Until recently, the record at Glacier National Park was somewhat the same. The area was established as a national park in 1911. There were no deaths from grizzlies until the fatal night of August 13, 1967. On that night two girls were killed in campgrounds separated by some twenty miles. In his most readable and well written account of that tragedy, *The Night of the Grizzlies,* Jack Olsen says that a computer estimated that the probability of such a double attack was on the order of one chance in a trillion. One bear in particular had been observed during the summer raiding a garbage dump and acting in a most ungrizzly fashion. He appeared often in daylight; sometimes when he was enraged by noise or an unfamiliar sound he would hurl himself against the cabin. We will probably never know all the facts of the deaths of two young harmless girls. Enos Mills realized, however, that among grizzlies there are renegades and outlaws as well as lovable old milktoasts. He wanted to present a case for the maligned majority.

There is considerable controversy about control of the bears near the garbage dumps of campgrounds. Some maintain that the bears (grizzlies in particular) should be trapped and removed to a more remote spot where plenty of their natural food is available. Others maintain that the bears have become dependent on this food supply, and have lost their natural foraging abilities. They suggest a gradual weaning away from what is an essentially undesirable situation for either the bears or the public.

But *The Grizzly* is more than a book about an animal. It was written by a naturalist who is gradually becoming better known outside his adopted state of Colorado. Enos Mills was born near Kansas City, Kansas in 1870. In 1886 he settled in a cabin at the foot of Long's Peak in the Colorado Rockies. There he was to spend most of the rest of his life. A self-educated man, he was a dedicated naturalist. He built Longs Peak Inn near his original cabin and to it came thousands of tourists. Before the creation of the National Park, Mills had not only led hearty groups up Longs Peak (which he climbed over 300 times in his life) but he also took bus loads of sightseers into the lower meadows and moraines of what is now the National Park.

He has been called the John Muir of the Rockies, the father of Rocky Mountain National Park. Enos A. Mills had served the federal government as a consultant and lecturer on forestry for several years, and at the same time he undertook snow measurements in the high country for the state of Colorado, and assiduously wrote numerous articles on the Rocky Mountains. Through his various lectures and articles, Mills continued to press for the establishment of a national park in the Rockies near the small village of Estes Park. My father, who met Enos Mills early that Spring, described him as a small, rather ordinary looking man, but more knowledgeable about that part of the country than anyone else.

But despite Mill's experience, knowledge and dedication, his efforts were to bring him a double-edged sword—of success (in the formation of the National Park), and personal tragedy.

His quarrel with the United States Government was over the question of the granting of a monopoly to a transportation company with exclusive rights within the National Park. He not only lost this battle, he also saw a monopoly given to another, and his own activities as guide rendered useless—and illegal. This man who had given thirty years of his life to the region was not about to be stopped by the new guardians of the wilderness and he continued to lead parties of tourists into the Park. He was warned, and finally cited for breaking the law. Shortly thereafter he embarked on another crusade across the country. On this tour he was injured in an accident on a subway in New York City. He returned to his retreat in the Rockies and died there eight months later, in September, 1922, some say of a broken heart.

So it is that in this fascinating narrative by Enos A. Mills, now available to the public again through Comstock Editions, we are able to take stock of two remarkable creatures, for surely this book is about two splendid creations of nature, each observing the other, each with respect for the other, each free. We can only regret that we haven't, at this point in time, a means of having the grizzly's account of Enos A. Mills.

Berkeley, California
March 2, 1973

INDEX